The Life
and Legend
of Tom Mix

The Life
and Legend
of Tom Mix

Paul E. Mix

South Brunswick and New York: A. S. Barnes and Company
London: Thomas Yoseloff Ltd

A. S. Barnes and Co., Inc.
Cranbury, New Jersey 08512

Thomas Yoseloff Ltd
108 New Bond Street
London W1Y OQX, England

Library of Congress Cataloging in Publication Data

Mix, Paul E.
  The life and legend of Tom Mix.

  Bibliography: p.
  1. Mix, Tom, 1880-1940. I. Title.
PN2287.M65M48   791.43′028′0924 [B]   71-146780
ISBN 0-498-07881-7

Printed in the United States of America

to
my loving wife, Dixie,
and our children, Donna, Linda, and Tom.

Contents

Preface

Tom Mix was a man of boundless energy and ambition. By the time he was forty years of age, he was one of the top ten box office attractions in this country. Tom Mix and his horse, Tony, flashed across the silver screen and into the hearts and minds of thousands of youngsters around the world.

It is difficult to say when Tom Mix began his rise to fame. Perhaps it was his destiny. One can say with certainty that it was as a boy that he first dreamed of going West and becoming a hero. It was also as a boy that he first learned to ride, rope, and shoot a handgun. Nevertheless, it was not until Tom had worked for the famed Miller Brothers' 101 Real Wild West Ranch that he became a cowhand in the real sense of the word.

To the older generation, Tom Mix will be remembered as the western super-hero in the white hat, who overcame all obstacles to defeat the forces of evil while protecting the innocence of the ranch foreman's daughter. To the younger generation, Tom Mix is at most a famous American whose name appears in The National Cowboy Hall of Fame and the World Book Encyclopedia. Yet, there is no doubt that Tom Mix was one of the most colorful characters of his time. His career was richly intermingled with the early history of wild west shows, rodeos, silent movies and traveling circuses.

The story of Tom Mix is an interesting one. It tells of the life of a man whose journeys took him from his humble birthplace in western Pennsylvania to the great plains of the southwest where he eventually gained great fame and fortune. It tells how one man became a living legend in his own time, and yet it tells of the trials and tribulations of a very human man with very human feelings.

It has been said that "History decides the greatness of a man."

Tom Mix clowning around with a mighty midget brigade. (Courtesy Tom Mix Museum)

"Look out, Pedro—here I come!" (Courtesy Tom Mix Museum)

"Who said I'd rather kiss my horse?" (Courtesy Tom Mix Museum)

This is particularly true in the case of Tom Mix, because his real life was often obscured by his legendary acts of heroism. To understand the man, we must study his life in the context of his time and not merely pass judgment on him, based on present-day standards.

This biography of Tom Mix has been compiled from numerous data sources. Documentary evidence was obtained from various government agencies, state historical societies, museums and libraries. In addition, many of Tom's personal friends, and a few old enemies, were interviewed. For the serious student of motion picture history, the Appendix contains a wealth of detailed information.

The Life
and Legend
of Tom Mix

My Wish For You

"May you brand your largest calf crop—
May your range grass never fail—
May your water holes stay open—
May you ride an easy trail.

"May you never reach for leather—
Nor your saddle horse go lame—
May you drop your loop on critters,
With your old unerring aim.

"May your stack of chips grow taller—
May your shootin' e'er stay true—
May good luck plumb snow you under—
Is always my wish for you."

by *Tom Mix*

1

Boyhood and Family

Each spring in the early 1800s, small bands of husky lumbermen poled rafts up the west branch of the Susquehanna River, from Lock Haven to Driftwood, Pennsylvania. Because of the shallow waters and tricky currents, families and friends would remain at home, waiting for the lumbermen to return with their annual harvest of logs from the great woodland forests. After the harvest, the huge logs would be floated down the Susquehanna to lumber mills in the Lock Haven area. As the lumber industry grew, it became more economical to build mills in the harvest areas and soon the lumbermen were homesteading picturesque Bennett's Valley, near Driftwood. Tom's great-great-grandfather, Amos Mix, and his family, were among the first to settle in the Driftwood area in 1804. The little hollow (a small valley between mountains) where the Mix family settled was later named Mix Run, as a tribute to Amos Mix.

Tom's father, Ed Mix, like his father and his father before him, continued to work as a lumberman in the scenic mountain forests. Ed was a teamster. He used a team of horses to drag logs out of the woods and haul them to nearby lumber mills in Hicks Run.

Lumbering in early times was a seasonal occupation reserved for the months from spring through fall. In the winter, snow piled up in the valleys and lightly covered the numerous creeks and streams, giving them the appearance of snowy roadways. Winter was the time for mending clothes and doing the numerous homestead chores which had been postponed during the working season. It was the time to get together with good friends around the cast-iron, pot-bellied stove. Because the menfolk were home, it was also a pretty good time for the women to have children.

Tom Mix made his entry into the world in the early morning hours on January 6, 1880. Mrs. Marshall Barr, the Mix's nearest neighbor, who lived about a half a mile away, was Mrs. Mix's midwife. Tom was born at home, in a little frame house located midway between the Pennsylvania Railroad Line and Bennett's Branch of the Susquehanna River. Tom's brother, Harry, age six, had trouble going to sleep the night before as the excitement of having a new baby sister or brother raced through him. Little sister, Emma, age three, wasn't even aware of the big event until hours after the fact. Several months earlier, Mrs. Mix had decided that if the child were a boy, she would name it after her grandfather, the Reverend Thomas Hollen. Reverend Hollen married Tom's mother and father and gave them the land on which they had built their home.

Tom's mother, whose maiden name was Elizabeth Smith, had lived in Harrisburg, Pennsylvania, as a young girl. Her grandmother, a widow, had met and later married the Reverend Thomas Hollen who was a widower. At the age of 14, Elizabeth went with her grandmother and grandfather to live in Driftwood. Elizabeth

The mansion: Home of John E. DuBois, Ed Mix's employer. (Author's collection)

Tom with his favorite girl: his mother. (Courtesy Frankie Barr Caldwell)

was a small woman of Pennsylvania Dutch ancestry. Ed Mix lived
near Reverend Hollen and eventually Ed and Elizabeth were married. Tom's father, Edwin E. Mix, always known as just plain Ed,
was born in Mix Run, Pennsylvania. Ed, of English and northern
Irish ancestry, was tall, with broad shoulders and a very muscular
build.

The mills that Ed worked for were owned by John E. DuBois,
an early-day giant in the lumber industry. When Tom was four
and his father 29, the family moved from Mix Run to Driftwood.
Driftwood was a larger town, situated more conveniently for Ed's
work. Tom attended school for the first time while the family was
living in Driftwood. The school was a small, one-room, frame building where reading, writing, and arithmetic were taught in the first
through sixth grades. Tom attended school for about two years

and then his family moved again. This time the Mix family moved to DuBois, Pennsylvania, at the request of the DuBois family. Tom was about eight years old at this time.

Ed's employment in DuBois came about as the result of Mrs. DuBois's efforts to remodel her home, *The Mansion*. While in the process of putting in lawns and gardens with walks, it was necessary, on one occasion, to back a wagon loaded with topsoil down a gently curved driveway. Whitmarsh, the family coachman at the time, was unable to back the wagon that distance without getting either the wheels of the wagon or the horses on the grass. This greatly displeased Mrs. DuBois, and Mr. DuBois promised to get her a more competent coachman. Mr. DuBois went to his woods' foreman and told him to send his best teamster to the house. The foreman sent Ed, because he was known to have an almost magical way with animals, especially horses. When Ed arrived, Mrs. DuBois told him what she wanted him to do. Ed backed the wagon down the long driveway without touching the grass with the horses' hoofs or the wagon's wheels, even though the team of horses was strange to him. This so pleased Mrs. DuBois that she asked Ed if he would move his family to DuBois and become the family coachman.

Mr. DuBois also loved horses and he owned the finest harness racing and driving stables in the DuBois area. After a short time, Mr. DuBois promoted Ed to the job of superintendent of the stables. Tom seemed to inherit his love of horses from his father. He was always hanging around the stables, making a nuisance out of himself and always wanting a ride.

According to Tom's mother, Tom was about nine when he had his first unusual riding experience. It seems that as a boy one of Tom's early chores was to put the family cow out to pasture and to bring her home in the evening. On this particular evening, Mrs. Mix just happened to look out the window in time to see young Tom coming in a downpour with his umbrella opened, riding on the back of the cow. Tom was taking the easy way home and he didn't get his feet muddy, but Mrs. Mix was quick to put an end to that type of riding.

Tom had continued with his elementary schooling in DuBois, but he wasn't a good student. His older sister Emma was an outstanding student and Tom just wasn't able to follow in her footsteps. He would sit for hours staring out the window, just plain daydreaming. Finally, after completing the fourth grade, Tom decided to quit school. Tom loafed around the stables, did a few chores for

Tom inherited his love of horses from his father. (Ed Mix on Tony Jr.) (Courtesy Frankie Barr Caldwell)

Tom's parents were treated like visiting royalty. (Courtesy Frankie Barr Caldwell)

the family, and picked up what odd jobs he could. In those days, it was common for children to drop out of school before completing the sixth grade.

Then one day, when Tom was about ten, something happened that changed the whole course of his life. Buffalo Bill and his Wild West Show came to the Clearfield Fairgrounds, which were next to the DuBois Racetrack. The show featured Buffalo Bill (William F. Cody), Annie Oakley (Phoebe Mozee), and a host of cowboys and Indians, who performed stunt after stunt, displaying their skills with knives, lariats, and guns. Tom and his friends were set afire with the adventure and romance of the "Old West." Tom had never before seen anything so exciting as a Wild West Show. For the first time in his life, he wanted to go West to become a sheriff and defend the frontier against outlaws. After the Wild West Show, Tom and his friends made lariats of their own and raced about the racetrack, on imaginary horses, roping each other.

With the passing of time, some of the boys lost their interest in the Wild West; but Tom never did. One afternoon Tom got together with his friend the blacksmith and fashioned a set of homemade throwing knives. After Tom figured he was quite proficient with them, he decided to try out his new act. Since mother wasn't home, he borrowed her best linen tablecloth and hung it on the wall. He asked his assistant, little sister Esther, age seven, to stand perfectly still in front of the tablecloth. Tom threw the first knife a bit to the right of her and was proceeding to pin the rest of the knives around her, when who should walk in, but mother. Again, Mrs. Mix interfered with young Tom's career and dad made it difficult for him to sit down for a while.

Tom was only twelve when he felt the sting of his first bullet wound. He and his pal, Denny Dwyer, had been doing a little target shooting with an old, single-shot pistol that Tom had bought from his savings. One of the cartridges stuck going into the chamber and Denny pulled out his pocketknife to remove it. As the two boys were bent over the gun, it discharged. The bullet lodged in Tom's left leg just above the knee. Tom decided to dig for the bullet with Denny's knife, but it soon became apparent that he was doing more harm than good. Tom gave the knife back to Denny and tied an old rag bandage around his leg. When he got home, he told his mother what had happened and she looked for the bullet but couldn't find it. She cleaned the wound and bandaged Tom's leg. The leg healed up fine and it wasn't until 25 years later,

Tom gave his parents a new automobile on Ed's 72nd birthday. (Courtesy Frankie Barr Caldwell)

when the leg started to give him trouble, that the bullet was found and removed.

For awhile Tom didn't see much of Denny, for Tom's mother more or less blamed Denny for the accident. However, in a month or so, Tom talked his mother into giving him his gun back, and soon he and Denny were back shooting at their familiar cork, bottle, and nail-head targets. Tom's mother didn't like his playing with guns, but she gave into his desire to shoot because she knew that he loved guns and was an exceptionally good shot for his age. Mrs. Mix believed and trusted her son when he promised to be more careful.

The saying goes that "Tom learned to ride anything that could walk" during those formative years in DuBois. He rode work horses, mules, and stable ponies. He practiced mounts and dismounts, riding bareback, and standing on a galloping horse. One of his favorite stunts was standing on a galloping horse while it raced toward an open barn door. Horse and rider were too tall to clear the barn door opening; so just as the horse started into the barn, Tom would jump into a stack of hay piled next to the barn door.

Tom also continued to practice with his lariat and gun. He lassoed fence posts, hitching posts, and all sorts of inanimate objects. But his first real roping experience came when he was fourteen. One afternoon at the DuBois stockyards, he tied one end of his lariat around his waist and then he proceeded to rope a prize bull with the other end. The frightened animal took off, dragging Tom behind. Finally, after being beaten and bruised by the rough ground, he was rescued by one of the stockmen. Tom was discouraged but he didn't give up. After his recovery, the first glimpse that friends got of him was when he walked down North Brady Street with his lariat in hand, lassoing empty hitching posts.

Tom's second cousin, Warren Mix, was shot to death in the driveway of Tom's birthplace home when Tom was fourteen. The shooting embittered many members of the Mix family, including Tom's grandfather, Solomon. The circumstances leading up to the shooting were as follows:

The original Mix farm settled by Amos was handed down to his son, James, when Amos died. James kept the ownership of the farm until he had grown old and helpless and was deeply in debt. James's sons—Hezikiah, Solomon, Henry, and James J.—cut and sold timber to pay off the debt. Ownership of the farm was then turned over to the sons, who after a number of years again went into debt, causing the farm to be sold for taxes.

Two men, Apker and Clark, who lived in Grant, Pennsylvania, bought the farm when it was sold for taxes. Warren Mix, Henry's son, also lived in Grant and wanted to buy the farm, but his home mysteriously burned to the ground. Warren and his wife, Cora, moved back to Mix Run after their house burned and rented some rooms at the McQuay house. Warren, suspicious about how his house burned and resentful that he could not now afford to buy the old Mix farm, vowed that he would kill Apker or Clark or anyone else, if they tried to "turn a furrow" (plow) on the land.

Early on the morning of April 27, 1894, Clark visited Marshall Barr of Mix Run and had breakfast with him and his family. During the course of his conversation with them, Clark asked Marshall if he would plow the old Mix farm for him that spring. Marshall said he wouldn't and explained that Warren had threatened to shoot anyone who attempted to farm the land. Marshall said that he didn't want to get involved in any sort of dispute with Warren.

After breakfast, Marshall left to help Frank Smith, a neighbor, float some logs across a nearby creek before the spring floods came. Clark left to visit DeGarmo, another neighbor of Marshall's, to see if he would plow the old Mix farm. (DeGarmo had bought the house that Tom was born in after Tom's family moved to Drift-wood.)

Clark was walking up the driveway, in front of DeGarmo's house, when he met Warren headed the other way. Warren threw some rocks at Clark and Clark ran to DeGarmo's house to try to borrow a gun. DeGarmo wouldn't give Clark a gun, so Clark ran on to the next house, which was owned by a family named Moats. Moats

Tom's mother and father lived a comfortable, commonplace life in DuBois, as their only living son climbed to stardom's pinnacle. (Courtesy Tom Mix Museum)

gave Clark a gun and Clark headed back toward DeGarmo's drive-way.

When Clark returned to the driveway, Warren was sitting there, on an old stump fence,[1] waiting for Clark. Warren had a club in his hand that had a four inch burr[2] screwed on the end of it. As Clark approached, Warren rushed at him and raised the club. Clark fired the gun and Warren fell to the ground, dead. Marshall Barr and Frank Smith heard the shot and came running. When they got to the scene, Clark told them what he had done and he showed them the bruises on his face where he claimed that Warren had hit him with stones. Clark surrendered himself to Marshall Barr and Frank Smith.

During the trial, Warren's lawyer tried to prove that Clark had shot Warren and committed cold blooded murder because of the odd location where the bullet had entered Warren's vest. Warren's lawyer contended that Warren had turned away when he saw that Clark had a gun, thus trying to avoid the fight. George Huntley, Clark's lawyer, took Warren's club and raised it as if to strike the jury. When he did this, the buttons on his vest were brought into view in a location similar to that where the bullet had struck Warren. The jury was convinced that Warren had been the aggressor and Clark was convicted on a lesser charge of manslaughter. Clark was sentenced to a few years of imprisonment because of the fact that Warren did not have a gun and it was not necessary for Clark to have returned to the driveway for a confrontation.

Warren was dead, at the age of 31, and eventually the old Mix farm was plowed, but not by Clark. Because of the shooting, the farm was resold, this time to the Moats family. Now, the Mix family disliked the Moats family even more than they had disliked Clark because one of the Moats family gave Clark the gun to shoot Warren and then had become the ones who ended up with the old Mix farm. For a while, it was a minor miracle that a full-scale feud didn't erupt between the Mix family and the Moats family.

Tom made one important observation, right or wrong, concerning the events leading up to Warren's death. Tom saw his family as a group of poor, hard-working lumbermen who had lost their family homestead after 90 years, and he saw John E. DuBois, a millionaire, as a happy man who had just about everything in life. Tom made

1. Fence made by stretching wire from tree stump to tree stump.
2. Sharp metal object.

The earliest known picture (1888) of Tom Mix (1st row, 3rd from right); he was in the third grade and was about eight years old. (Courtesy Tom Mix Museum)

up his mind that one day he too would have great material wealth. This desire to "be somebody" and "have the finer things of life" became a major driving force in his life.

In his mid-teens, Tom was rough and tough and he loved outdoor sports. Tom was tall and broad-shouldered; he was a big boy for his age. One of Tom's favorite sports was football, and even though he had quit school at an early age, he did play football with the DuBois High School team. In those days, there were no scholastic requirements for football and it was common to recruit boys right off the street in preparation for a big game. Tom was frequently appointed team captain because he had natural leadership abilities, and besides, his mother had one of the few sewing machines in the

David Waite Mix, who was about 10 years older than Tom, thought that Tom was selfish as a boy because he put his boyhood dreams and ambitions above all else (1894). (Author's collection)

area. Tom and his mother made football uniforms for the team and Tom even made his first western outfit with mother's help. One Saturday after Thanksgiving Day, 1896, Tom, and three friends from the town of State College, joined the high school team to play in an exhibition game of All-Stars. Tom led his team to a one-sided 21-0 victory.

Tom also like to play baseball and go bicycle riding. The bicycle was Tom's chief mode of transportation around town. Bicycle racing was also a very popular sport in the 1890s. One day Tom read in the newspapers that there was to be a big bicycle race in Hartford, Connecticut on July 4, 1897. The first prize was to be a large sterling silver coffee pot, with charcoal warmer and matching silver cup. Tom couldn't resist trying to win a prize like that. For weeks he practiced for the big event by riding his bicycle up and down the hills around DuBois. When the time grew near, Tom and his bicycle boarded a train and headed toward Hartford. Tom stayed with relatives while he was in Hartford and they turned out to see Tom walk away with the first prize trophy.

Later, after Tom returned home, Tom's mother found a note in his room and learned just how determined her son had been about that bicycle race. On the note, Tom had written, "Whatever you do, do it better than anyone else!" Tom had gained confidence that he would accomplish great things if he put forth his every effort.

Reflecting on his boyhood in later life, Tom himself remarked, "My first boyhood dreams were when I was learning to ride a horse. My desire at that time was to be a top-notch sheriff in the West where a man had to be a man. I dreamed and imagined that way of life as far back as I can remember. That was the world I lived in. I imagined all sorts of dangerous traps and figured out ways to get away from my imaginary enemies. Unknowingly, I was schooling myself from the first grade up, because as a young man, I ended up in the West. I felt ready and qualified when the time came— and the time did come when I was a sheriff."

About her own son, Mrs. Mix often remarked, "As a boy, Tom was just a big devil, too busy playing with guns to learn much." That sentiment was shared by many of Tom's friends and relatives. He didn't earn their respect as a boy because, in that day and age, a boy was expected to do a man's labor. They thought his boyhood dreams were a waste of his talents and abilities.

After Tom became famous, he continued to help his family when money was needed for medical expenses, etc. Tom frequently visited his parents in DuBois, and he sent his mother money almost monthly. Tom also treated his parents to an extended vacation in California and later, for Ed's 72nd birthday, he bought his parents their first automobile. Tom also helped his younger sister, Esther, get a job with the wardrobe section of a large California film studio after her husband, Dr. F. H. Bell, died.

Tom's rise to fame brought about only one minor problem. Mrs. Mix, like any normal mother, was very proud of her son. She talked and talked about him until even some of her closest friends got fed up about hearing of Tom. Her words began to go in one ear and out the other, and as a result only a few of Tom's boyish pranks were remembered for very long.

With the exception of Esther, all of Tom's immediate family lived out their lives in DuBois. Tom's brother, Harry, died at age 16 and was buried in the old Rumberger Cemetery near DuBois. Few of Tom's friends knew Harry because he died shortly after the family moved to DuBois. Tom's father, Edwin E. Mix, died on November 29, 1927, at age 73, and his mother, Elizabeth, died July 25, 1937, at age 79. His older sister, Mrs. Emma Yoder Swartz, died June 19, 1959, at age 82.

2

Black Powder and Heavy Artillery

The Spanish-American War of 1898 was a popular war with the American people. American newspapers published sensational accounts of Spanish misrule and oppression. These stories tended to unite the American people in their desire to overthrow the Spanish rule and help the Cuban revolutionaries. A few American expansionists still hoped to acquire Cuba through annexation.

In November 1897, President McKinley demanded that Spain grant Cuba at least limited self-government but the Cuban revolutionaries would not accept anything less than total independence, so they continued their fight. Pro-Spanish factions in Cuba violently protested America's political intervention and they began to riot against Americans in Havana. The battleship *Maine* was allegedly sent to Havana to protect American lives. It mysteriously exploded in Havana Harbor on February 15, 1898, killing 260 persons. The sinking of the *Maine* was the catalyst that solidly united the American people against Spain.

With the sinking of the battleship, great excitement swept through all parts of the country. "Remember the *Maine*" became a national slogan and eighteen-year-old Tom Mix and his friends were immediately caught up in the tide of patriotism. On April 25, 1898, war was officially declared against Spain. Some of Tom's friends joined the Navy; others boarded a train for Washington, D.C., where they enlisted through the General Recruiting Service.

On April 26, 1898, the day after war was declared, Thomas E.

The sinking of the Maine *in Havana Harbor united American sentiment against Spain. The wreck of the battleship is depicted here. (Library of Congress photo)*

Mix enlisted at Washington Barracks, D. C., and was assigned to Battery M, 4th Regiment United States Artillery.[1] Tom apparently told three little white lies when he gave his middle initial as "E.," his birthplace as Driftwood, and his birthdate as January 6, 1877. One can hardly blame Tom for using his father's name, Edwin, in preference to his real middle name, Hezikiah.[2] It is hard to picture any young man going through the service being called Hezikiah or maybe just plain "Hezzy." Likewise, Driftwood was the closest town of any size to Mix Run, his actual birthplace. Tom seems to have lied about his age because he looked older than 18, his mother did not want him to join the service, and his elders generally associated the magic number, 21, with the age of manhood.

Tom's first assignment with Battery M was to guard the DuPont powder works at Montchanin, Delaware. During the Spanish-American War, the DuPont powder mills were the major producer of

1. Based on information from the National Archives.
2. From the Cameron County Census of 1880.

Tom as a private in the Artillery. (Courtesy Tom Mix Museum)

cocoa powder or brown powder for the U. S. government. In April and May 1898, Battery M guarded the powder mills against the possibility of sabotage. There was also the possibility that an attacking naval force might attempt to sail up the Delaware River to attack Wilmington or Philadelphia. Battery M made their camp in the upper powder yards, which were known as the Upper Yards or Eleutherian Mills.

Tom's first assignment with Battery M 4th Regimental Artillery was to guard the DuPont Powder Works at Montchanin, Delaware. (Courtesy Eleutherian Mills–Hadley Foundation)

Lower drying house, Hagley Yard, showing workmen and horsedrawn power magazine (1895). (Courtesy Eleutherian Mills–Hagley Foundation)

Powder Mills in the lower yard, before 1893. (Courtesy Eleutherian Mills–Hagley Foundation)

U.S. Troops on guard at DuPont's Carney's Point, New Jersey, facility during the Spanish-American War. (Courtesy Eleutherian Mills–Hagley Foundation)

At the start of hostilities, DuPont was asked by the government to produce 5 million pounds of brown prismatic powder as quickly as possible. Smokeless powder was not yet being produced in large quantities. At the outbreak of the war, production in the Brandywine mills was 3000 pounds of powder a day; after going onto wartime production, this figure increased within sixty days to a daily output of 25,000 pounds. Within four months, DuPont had delivered 2.2 million pounds, most of it going to the Navy. DuPont powder shipments were usually sent to the Schuylkill and Frankford arsenals and protected en route by military escorts.

Late in May 1898, Battery M was relieved of guard duty by the First Battalion of the Second Regiment of Pennsylvania Volunteers. Because of the fear of an attack on Philadelphia by Admiral Cervera and the Spanish fleet, Battery M was ordered to take up stations at Battery Point, Delaware[3] and Fort Delaware on Pea Patch Island. The Delaware River was protected by eight-inch guns at Fort Mott, New Jersey, and Battery Point, Delaware. Three 12-inch disappearing guns at Fort Delaware on Pea Patch Island were aimed

3. Battery Point was later known as Fort DuPont.

Tom was promoted to Corporal in September 1898. (Courtesy Tom Mix Museum)

directly down river. Fort Delaware was also the mine control center. The duties of Battery M consisted of drilling and practice firing of the 12-inch guns. It was a nerve-racking vigil, waiting for an attack which never came.

Tom continued to perform his routine battery and post duties at Fort DuPont until the end of the war. He had served intermittent assignments at the DuPont Powder Works, Fort Delaware, Washington Barracks, and Battery Point and was promoted to the rank of Corporal in September 1898. Tom regretted missing out on the action, but in reality, the Spanish-American war lasted only a few short months.

On the first of May, Commodore George Dewey, who had sailed from Hong Kong to Manila Bay, destroyed a Spanish fleet of 10 ships. There was no loss of life or serious damage to the American fleet. At the same time, Rear Admiral William T. Sampson began a partial blockade of Cuba and continued scouting the Caribbean Sea for the second Spanish fleet, which had left Spain under Admiral Pascual Cervera. Cervera's fleet was finally located at landlocked Santiago Harbor and blockaded on May 28, 1898. Admiral Cervera tried to run the American blockade on July 3, 1898, and again the entire Spanish fleet was quickly beached or destroyed by the pursuing American fleet.

Tom's outfit, Battery M of the 4th Regiment U. S. Artillery, was a heavy artillery unit and as such saw no action during the Spanish-American War. Heavy artillery units were used only to guard the eastern coast against the possibility of attack or retaliation. On the other hand, light or field artillery units, such as Light Battery B, could be mobilized quickly enough to support ground actions. Light Battery B of the 4th Regiment, under the command of Captain William R. Anderson, did participate in the landings and skirmishes in Cuba and Puerto Rico in June and July, 1898.[4]

The big land battle of the Spanish-American War was the battle for Kettle and San Juan Hills which took place on July 1, 1898. The Spanish defenses on these hills had to be taken in order to completely isolate Santiago. By nightfall of the same day, there were about 1600 American casualties, but the defenses had been captured. American newspapers quickly heralded Colonel Wood and Lt. Colonel Theodore Roosevelt as America's heroes of the conflict, but it was not until July 17, 1898, that the besieged city of Santiago surrendered.

As a result of the war, Spain granted Cuba its freedom and the United States had established itself as a world power. Under the Treaty of Paris, signed on December 10, 1898, Spain ceded Guam, Puerto Rico, and the Philippines to the United States, and in return the United States paid $20 million to Spain for public lands in the

4. From 4th Artillery Regimental Returns.

U.S. Regulars at Fort Monroe eating last "mess" before leaving for the South and Cuba. (From an original stereo photo by J. F. Jarvis, 1898.) (Courtesy Library of Congress)

Philippines. Despite the victory, many Americans disapproved of our expansionist policies.

The Spanish-American War ended even more abruptly than it had started. Just when the wheels of industry were churning, they had to be brought to a screeching halt. Government orders for supplies were cancelled and most of the soldiers found themselves with two additional years of service to fulfill before their three-year enlistments were up.

Tom Mix remained with Battery M until April 17, 1899, when he accepted a transfer to Battery O of the same regiment. With the transfer came a promotion to the rank of Sergeant. Sergeant Mix was stationed at Fort Monroe, Virginia, which had been the receiving center for the wounded returning from the Spanish-American War. Fort Monroe was now the primary training center for the Artillery. The National Soldier's Home, which had also served as a hospital during the war, was located a short distance from the fort. Tom helped train recruits, visited with the old timers at the Home, and took part in remodeling activities for the next several months. The remodeling activities consisted of making the fort's living quarters more habitable and upgrading the armament. The Army had learned one lesson from the Spanish-American War: it was not prepared for a major conflict!

While Tom was at Fort Monroe, the Philippine Insurrection reared its ugly head. Tom was busier than a cat on a hot tin roof until August 5, 1899, when the fort had to be evacuated due to an outbreak of Yellow Fever at the National Soldier's Home. The battery left Fort Monroe by steamer and headed for Fort Terry, New York. The battery returned to Fort Monroe a month later, after the threat of Yellow Fever had subsided. Duties returned to normal until February 8, 1900, when the battery went by steamer to Washington, D. C., to attend the funeral of Major General Henry Lawton. The battery returned to their posts two days later.

On June 25, 1900, Battery O left Fort Monroe, Virginia, to take up permanent stations at Fort Hancock, New Jersey. Tom was promoted to a First Sergeant on November 13, 1900, and he took his first furlough and returned to his home in DuBois, Pennsylvania. As a First Sergeant, Tom was the highest ranking non-commissioned officer in his battery. His battery consisted of a Captain, First Lieutenant, Second Lieutenant, First Sergeant, three regular Sergeants, and approximately 100 enlisted men. The enlisted men under Tom respected him; most of them considered him a natural leader and a nice guy. One of his comrades later remarked, "Tom was all man and you'd better stay on the right side of him."

The Philippine Insurrection ended in March 1901, and First Sergeant Thomas E. Mix was honorably discharged at Fort Hancock on April 25, 1901. However, the Boer War, which had started in

January 1900, was still going strong, so Tom immediately reenlisted. Tom took 15 days of furlough and returned to Fort Monroe to visit with old friends. While in the Norfolk area, Tom met an attractive schoolteacher named Grace Allin. Grace was Tom's first love and Tom knew that she was the right girl for him. Tom's 15-day furlough soon ended and for the first time in his life, Tom found himself really hating to have to return to the fort.

Exactly what happened to Tom for the next year is not known. There were rumors that the Army let some of their regulars go to volunteer to help the Boers. However, there are no entries in Battery O's History of Events Records to indicate that this actually happened. Officially, Tom performed his routine battery and post duties at Fort Hancock until July 12, 1902, when he took his next furlough.

Tom returned to Norfolk during his next furlough. Tom and Grace had been separated for a little over a year and to the two young lovers it seemed like an eternity. They had written to each other, of course, but nothing short of being with each other could fulfill the yearning they shared. Tom and Grace decided that they shouldn't postpone their marriage any longer. They went to Louisville to announce the good news to Grace's parents.

Thomas E. Mix and Grace I. Allin were married on July 18, 1902, by Ed Meglemry, Justice of the Peace.[5] Grace's mother and sister, Belle and Bernice, were witnesses to the ceremony. Grace's father, a furniture dealer in the Louisville area, didn't attend the wedding. If his little girl was happy, that was all that mattered. Tom and Grace had about 12 days of furlough left for their honeymoon.

Tom was at the fort for a little less than three months before Grace began questioning the wisdom of being married to a professional soldier. She soon learned that absence didn't make the heart grow fonder. She couldn't see any sense to being a soldier when there wasn't a war going on. For all practical purposes, the Boer War had ended in May 1902 and the country was enjoying a period of relative peace. Grace made life pretty tough for Tom when she asked him to decide whether he wanted the Army or her.

On October 20, 1902, First Sergeant Thomas E. Mix took his last furlough. He gave his expected destination as Pittsburgh. It is doubtful that he went there and it is even more doubtful that he ever expected to return to Fort Hancock. On October 25, 1902, Tom's furlough expired and he was listed as AWOL. The AWOL

5. Book #7, Page #20, Jefferson County Court Records.

As a First Sergeant, Tom was the highest ranking non-commissioned officer in his battery. (Courtesy Tom Mix Museum)

period ended on November 4, 1902, and Tom Mix was officially listed as a deserter in his regimental returns. Tom was never apprehended or returned to military control, and therefore he never received a court-martial for that offense or a discharge for his second enlistment.

Tom's commanding officer never issued a warrant for his arrest.

During this time in history, the Army seems to have been content merely to let the matter drop. Regimental records show that desertion did increase after the war and fewer entries are made with regard to deserters being returned to Army custody and prosecution.

Tom's desertion had a great impact on his life. First of all, he was never quite sure whether the Army was still looking for him or not. Partly because he had always wanted to go West and partly because he was on the run, he and Grace moved into the southwest late in 1902. They settled in Guthrie, Oklahoma, which was then the capital of the Oklahoma Territory. For a short time, Grace continued her work as an English teacher and Tom taught a class in physical fitness. Grace's father did not like the idea of his daughter being married to an Army deserter and eventually he was successful in having his daughter's marriage annulled. For the next ten years, Tom is described as "the type of person who never volunteered much information about his past."

Late in 1927, a long time after Tom had gained national fame as a western silent motion picture star, he applied for membership in the United Spanish War Veterans organization. James J. Murphy, Quartermaster General of that organization, wrote to the Adjutant General, U. S. Army, and requested information pertaining to Tom's service in Batteries M and O of the 4th U. S. Artillery. All the pertinent facts relating to Tom's service were given to the United Spanish War Veterans and Tom was given a life membership in that organization, belonging to Joe Wheeler Camp No. 5, U.S.W.V., Prescott, Arizona.

The question of Tom's desertion came up again at the time of his death. His estate tried to secure an American Flag from the Veteran's Administration for the casket during his funeral. The Veteran's Administration hesitated to supply the flag and John Ford of Hollywood fame intervened for the family and wrote to the V.A. and U.S.W.V. Ford was a relative of the Quartermaster General of the United Spanish War Veterans. In regard to Mr. Ford's letter, the U.S.W.V. replied, "Confidentially, I wish to advise that Tom Mix evidently, in the days of his youth, was a soldier of fortune and just seemed to want to be in everybody's war. He had an honorable discharge from the war service and was mustered out in 1901 as a First Sergeant. He enlisted again a few days later and then, as you remember, the Boer War was starting and Tom left without saying 'Good-bye' to Uncle Sam."

Tom's marriage to Miss Allin and the circumstances leading up

Photograph that probably inspired the legend that Tom was one of Teddy Roosevelt's Rough Riders. (Courtesy Tom Mix Museum)

to his desertion were not generally known, and his desertion appears to have been excused on the basis that "he was off to fight another war." A simple check of the paperwork would of however revealed that he did not desert until October 1902, long after the Boer hostilities had ceased. For all practical purposes, the Boer War ended with the Treaty of Vereeniging, which was signed at Pretoria on May 31, 1902.

With regard to Tom's foreign service and the possibility that he was wounded in action, the National Archives and Records Service wrote, "Nothing has been found to show that Sergeant Mix served in any troop of the 1st Regiment United States Volunteer Cavalry, which was popularly known as Colonel Theodore Roosevelt's 'Rough Riders' or served beyond the continental limits of the United States. Medical or other records do not show that he was wounded in action. His name does not appear on the Index to the Decoration and Awards Correspondence of the Quartermaster General's Office. This indicates that he was not awarded any decorations or medals."

A similar check of Army Records in England revealed that no documentary evidence exists to indicate that Tom Mix ever served officially or unofficially in the Boer War.

At this point, it might be appropriate to ask, "Was the Thomas E. Mix, who deserted the Army on October 25, 1902, and the Tom Mix of Hollywood fame, one and the same?" Circumstantial evidence appears to be quite conclusive on this point. Thomas E. Mix was the only Tom or Thomas in the service at this time. When enlisting, Tom gave his birthplace as Driftwood, Pennsylvania. Driftwood was the closest town of any size to Mix Run, his actual birthplace. On November 13, 1900, First Sergeant Thomas E. Mix took a furlough to DuBois, Pennsylvania, where his parents were living. Photographs exist showing the monogram TEM on the former movie star's shirts. Some of these shirts can be seen at the Tom Mix Museum in Dewey, Oklahoma. Tom Mix himself admitted that he had served in Batteries M and O of the 4th Regiment Artillery, when applying for membership to the United Spanish War Veteran's organization.

It is curious that the Army appeared to be content to let the desertion charge drop and not pursue the matter. Tom was a First Sergeant at the time, which made him "top dog" with respect to the rest of the enlisted men. Aside from moving to Oklahoma Territory, Tom seems to have done little to evade the Army. He appears to have used the name Thomas E. Mix throughout his life.

3

The Years Before Fame

Tom Mix and Grace moved into the southwest for the first time late in 1902. Grace became an English teacher in Guthrie, Oklahoma, and Tom taught a physical fitness class. While in Guthrie, Tom had the pleasure of meeting Thompson B. Ferguson, the Governor of the Oklahoma Territory.[1] The Governor shared Tom's enthusiasm for working with young people and developing a physical fitness program to strengthen youth. Tom impressed the Governor with his Tom Sawyer flamboyance; his personality was his greatest asset.

After his marriage to Grace was annulled, Tom was disheartened and depressed. With the Governor's help and encouragement, Tom accepted a job as a drum major of the Oklahoma Cavalry Band, despite the fact that he was neither a member of the militia nor a musician. Tom proved to be a colorful and dashing figure as a drum major, bedecked in lace and gold braid. Tom and the Oklahoma Cavalry Band attended the St. Louis World's Fair in 1904 to help dedicate the laying of the cornerstone of the Oklahoma Building. Local newspapers mentioned Tom: "The handsome drum major, marching in the foreground, was a gallant figure who attracted a great deal of attention, especially from the ladies."

Will Rogers was also at the St. Louis World's Fair as a rodeo clown for the Colonel Zack Mulhall Wild West Show. There was one year's difference in the ages of Will and Tom and the two men soon became great friends. It was at the fair that Will Rogers

1. *Oklahoma City Times* obituary.

Will Rogers became Tom's friend at the 1904 St. Louis World's Fair. (Author's collection)

Tom Mix (front row, third from right) with Seth Bullock's "Cowboy Brigade." Washington, D. C., March 4, 1905. (Courtesy John M. Hall)

introduced a young girl of 14 to Tom Mix. Young Olive Stokes was very attractive and she was destined to one day become Tom's third wife.

Will Rogers started down the road to fame at the St. Louis World's Fair. During a show, a runaway steer from the Mulhall Wild West Show headed up the grandstand seats and into the crowd. Will ran into the stands, roped and tied the steer, and dragged him down the aisle by his tail. Stories about Will Rogers and the steer were widely publicized. The following season, the same stunt was performed by the Mulhall Wild West Show in New York's Madison Square Garden. This time the stunt was purposely staged and the steer was pushed through a rope fence leading to the grandstand area. Will ran into the stands, twirling his rope, and caught the steer. He slid the steer down the aisle and back into the arena. The announcer asked Will why he wouldn't let the steer stay in the grandstands and Will replied, "He doesn't have a ticket." As a result of the episode, Flo Ziegfeld hired Will to spin his rope and tell his yarns at the Ziegfeld Follies.

After the St. Louis World's Fair, Tom returned with the Oklahoma Cavalry Band to Oklahoma City, where the band appeared at the Delmar Gardens. Tom stayed in Oklahoma City after the band left, but he found it hard to find a good job. As he put it, "I came down here with the band to appear at the old Delmar Gardens and I stayed after the band left. The only thing that I could find to do was to be a bartender and I was always trying to find something else to do." It was during this period that Tom tried his hand at a number of occupations. He helped local law enforcement officers round up desperadoes and was a part-time ranch hand. When the seasonal work slacked up, he found himself returning to the bars in Oklahoma City.

In March 1905, Seth Bullock of Deadwood, South Dakota, formed the Cowboy Brigade to help celebrate the inauguration of President Theodore Roosevelt to a second term. The cowboys started from Edgemont, South Dakota, and traveled by train to Washington, D. C. and the White House. Tom joined the Brigade in Omaha as the train picked up riders and horses on its way East. The cowboys arrived in Washington, D. C. on March 4, 1905, which was then inauguration day. The Mulhall Wild West Show also went to the inauguration to provide western entertainment for the President and his friends. For Tom, it was an opportunity to renew many of the friendships he had made in St. Louis at the World's Fair.

The famed Miller Brothers trio who owned and operated the fabulous 101 Ranch southwest of Ponca City, Oklahoma. Left to right—Colonel Joseph C. Miller, who first hired Tom as a regular cowhand, Colonel George L. Miller, businessman, and Colonel Zack T. Miller, showman. (Author's collection)

After the inauguration, Tom returned to Oklahoma City and his job at the bar on Robinson Avenue. Tom lived in the Perrine Hotel and it was there that he first met Miss Kitty Jewel Perrine, the owner's daughter. Tom and Kitty were soon engaged, but Tom postponed their marriage several times in hopes of finding better employment.

It was while tending bar that Tom finally got the big break that he had been hoping for. One day, late in 1905, Colonel Joe Miller overheard Tom complaining of the inside work and expressing his desire to work outdoors. Colonel Joe Miller, along with his brothers George and Zack, owned and operated the famed Miller Brothers' 101 Real Wild West Ranch near Bliss, Oklahoma. Colonel Joe Miller hired Tom as a full-time cowboy for $15 per month, including room and board.

After landing the job with Miller, Tom and Kitty were married in the Perrine Hotel on December 20, 1905.[2] The Reverend Thomas Harper, pastor of the Pilgrim Congregational Church, performed the ceremony. H. M. Titton and Mrs. S. A. Eldridge were witnesses. Tom was 25 years old and Miss Kitty was 22.

Tom worked his first season for the 101 Real Wild West Ranch in 1906. His first job for the ranch was to act as a host for "dude" cowboys and cowgirls on vacation from the East. Colonel Zack Miller didn't think much of Tom as a cowboy. Tom looked the part however and proved himself to be an excellent host for the ranch. One oldtimer said, "Tom's duties at the ranch consisted mostly of just hanging around and looking pretty. He was not much of a cowboy as such when he first came to work for the 101. People use to say that Tom could get lost in an 800-acre pasture."

The cowboys who worked for the 101 Ranch were a rough bunch. They worked hard, played hard, and occasionally fought hard. They were the type of fellows who'd trip you coming out of the bunkhouse in order to beat you to the chow hall table. If you made it to the table, you still weren't safe. You'd have to make sure that one of your "buddies" didn't slip your chair out from under you before you could sit down. And if this wasn't bad enough, you might be punched in the mouth, if you tried to beat somebody else to a second helping.

If there was one thing that the 101 wasn't, it wasn't the ideal place for a young married couple. Many of the ranch hands never knew that Tom was married when he first came to work there. They did know that he dated a particular girl quite frequently. In any event, Tom and Kitty couldn't make a go of it and they were divorced. Kitty didn't like the idea of being married to a roustabout cowboy and Tom had no intentions of settling down and starting his own little family.

After the divorce, Tom turned his attentions to Miss Lucille Mulhall, Champion Cowgirl for the Mulhall Wild West Show. Colonel Zack Mulhall, Lucille's father, didn't approve of his daughter falling in love with a roustabout cowboy either, so he ran Tom off at gun point. Colonel Mulhall thought that a friend of his, who just happened to be a millionaire oil man from Burkburnett, Texas, would make a much better choice of a husband for Lucille.

At first, Tom didn't play an important part in the Miller Brothers'

2. Oklahoma County Court Records, Book 9, Page. 60.

Tom with 101 Ranch baseball team (1907). (Courtesy Jack C. Baskin)

Wild West Shows. Sometimes he was the dragman in the horsethief act. The "good guys" would hook a rope to a steel eye in the back of Tom's heavy leather jacket, pull him from his horse, and drag him around the arena, in front of the spectators. Tom didn't know it at the time, but he seems to have been completing his basic training for performing his own future stunts for the silver screen.

Tom was still acting as a host for the 101 Ranch in 1908, when E. W. Marland come to inspect the property. Ernest Whitworth Marland came to the 101 Ranch from Pennsylvania after learning about Oklahoma oil leases from a nephew. He had previously made over a million dollars with his discovery of the Congo Oil Field in West Virginia. Marland lost the money he had made in the business panic of 1907. While at the ranch, Marland collected samples of rock and shale, looking for signs of oil deposits. He found what he was looking for and the Marland Oil Company was formed. This company later became the 101 Oil Company and finally, Conoco. The familiar red triangle trademark, inspired by Marland's masonic ring, has survived to the present. As a result of the 101 Ranch oil

W. H. McFadden and E. W. Marland. McFadden was the financier and builder and Marland was the geologist and promoter who pioneered the oil industry in North Central Oklahoma. (Author's collection)

finding, Marland ended up making an estimated $85 million. Tom was now making $35 a month at the ranch and he never bothered to invest in the venture.

In December 1908, after Tom had finished his third season with the 101 Ranch and Wild West Show, he went to Dewey, Oklahoma, to see Olive Stokes. Olive had gone to Medora, North Dakota, to buy horses for her parent's ranch. Luke Bells, a foreman for the Stokes' Ranch, and Tom took a train to Medora to help Olive select the animals she was going to buy. Tom and Olive had a wonderful time together that Christmas. Olive stayed at the ranch of Nels and Katrine Nichols, who were friends of the Stokes family. After a farewell dance, held in Olive's honor, Olive and Tom were married by Nels Nichols, an authorized Justice of the Peace. Tom and Olive were married on January 19, 1909 and the newlyweds went to Miles City, Montana, for their honeymoon.[3]

After the honeymoon, Tom and Olive joined the Widerman Wild West Show in Amarillo, Texas. Tom's roping act was one of the top attractions. Unlike most of the cowboys, who used a 40-foot rope with a 25-foot reach, Tom used a 60-foot rope with a 40-foot reach. Things perked along fine until Tom asked Widerman for a raise and didn't get it. Tom and Olive decided to quit the Widerman Wild West Show in Denver, and organize their own show in Seattle.

Tom and Olive went to Seattle, where they hired a troop of 60 actors and performers. Charles Tipton and Ezra Black, friends of Tom, joined the show in Seattle. The Alaska-Yukon-Pacific Exposition was being held in Seattle that year and Tom's plan was to catch the overflow crowds from the exposition. They rented the Western Washington Fair Grounds and put on their own Wild West Show, which included a "days of olde" jousting act and mock battle with about 40 Blackfoot Indians.

A publicity photo was taken of Tom with a downed steer to help stimulate a little business. The picture was captioned, "Tom Mix, Champion Steer Thrower, A.Y.P.E., Seattle, Was. 1909." Business proved good when the weather was favorable, but the crowds failed to turn out when the weather was bad. The show was successful enough that three men attempted to rob Tom and Olive as the show was about to close. Tom and Olive foiled the attempt, but during the fracas, Tom was wounded in the hand.

After the successful conclusion of his own Wild West Show, Tom

3. Read *The Fabulous Tom Mix* by Olive Stokes Mix.

Tom Mix as the star of his own wild west show. (Author's collection)

and Olive joined Will A. Dickey's Circle D Wild West Show. Dickey was under contract to the Selig Polyscope Company of Chicago and he was deeply interested in motion pictures.

Tom returned to the Miller Brothers' Wild West Show late in 1910 and got into trouble with them for the first time. It seems that Tom borrowed a horse from the 101 Ranch to enter a rodeo in Oklahoma. Tom broke his leg in the rodeo and stabled the horse at the nearby Mulhall Ranch while he was in the hospital. The horse disappeared and Tom was charged with embezzlement. Bond was set at $1000, but it was never paid. Eventually, Tom cleared his good name and he agreed to appear with the Miller Brothers' Show while it was wintering in Mexico City.

While in Mexico City, Tom Mix, Stack Lee, and Bill Pickett staged the same stunt that started Will Rogers on the road to fame. The show was held at a Mexican Bullfight Ring and Tom and Stack turned a bull loose in the grandstands. Bill Pickett, with the aid of his pony, roped the bull and dragged him from the grandstands before he could do any damage. When the action started, the Miller Brothers quickly got up a bet with some Mexican officials that one of the boys would handle the situation in a specified period of time. Pickett beat the clock and the stunt allegedly netted the Miller boys $53,000. No one knows the amount of Tom's share of the loot, but he probably got a little bonus that year.

Tom was involved in one other incident at the 101 Ranch during the 1911 season. Jack Baskin and a little Mexican boy named Machacha were mascots of the 101 Wild West Show at the time. Both boys lived on the 101 Ranch property. Jack was ten years old at the time. His first cousin, Mabel Pettyjohn of Red Rock, Oklahoma, had married Colonel Zack Miller in 1906. Machacha had been adopted by Zack and Mabel when the 101 Show wintered in Mexico City in 1910. Machacha's parents had been lion tamers for a Mexican Circus and they were killed by the lions during one of their acts. One of Machacha's arms had been badly mangled by the lions when he attempted to pull his parents through the cage.

The two boys, Jack and Machacha, frequently played near the buffalo pens next to the Santa Fe Railroad. On this particular day, when the boys were out riding their Shetland ponies, they decided to dismount and coax a small buffalo calf to a large alfalfa hay stack to give him some better hay. The calf frequently crawled under the fence at the buffalo pen to browse around. This day was no different than any other except for the fact that the mother buffalo didn't like the boys pulling and tugging on her calf. In a fit of rage, the mother cow knocked down the gate of the buffalo pen and charged at the boys. The boys high-tailed it to the alfalfa stack with the cow close behind. Tom Mix, Stack Lee, and Bill Pickett, who were touring tenderfeet around the buffalo grounds, saw that the two boys were in trouble. Stack Lee wanted to shoot the cow but Tom said, "No, we'll rope her." Tom and Bill roped the cow and her calf and pulled them back into the buffalo pens. Stack helped too, of course, and the three men made temporary repairs to the gate as the boys looked on, admiringly. The three men were instant heroes as far as two young boys were concerned.

4

Sheriff Tom

Previously published stories about Tom Mix indicate that he was a Texas Ranger, Sheriff in Oklahoma and Kansas, and Deputy United States Marshal from 1905 through 1910. Most of these stories seem to be highly exaggerated, but it should be remembered that Tom was an excellent shot with a pistol and for this reason, his help could have been enlisted. As a bartender around the turn of the century, Tom was also in an excellent position to gather information about outlaws who frequently crossed state lines to avoid pursuit. Furthermore, Tom's work with the Wild West Shows and early movie producers was highly seasonal in nature, and would have left some time for him to act as a local law enforcement officer.

On September 22, 1905, Tom meandered down to Austin, Texas and signed up with the Company B Texas Ranger force.[1] Tom gave his birthplace as El Paso, Texas, and his occupation as ranchman. He enlisted under W. W. Sterling, Adjutant General, and Tom R. Hickman, Captain of the ranger force. Tom probably pulled a few strings to get a certificate with a perpetual enlistment. (W. W. Sterling was reputed to have been a friend of Tom's and a former Wild West Show performer.)

As a Texas Ranger, Tom allegedly brought the notorious Shonts brothers to justice. The Shonts brothers were cattle rustlers who plagued the citizens of Texas and New Mexico, spreading death

---

1. Based on Texas Ranger Certificate in Tom Mix Museum.

Tom demonstrates one way to "board" a train. (Courtesy Tom Mix Museum)

and destruction. Supposedly, Tom tracked the outlaws to their mountain hideout, was wounded in a gun battle with them, and held them captive until help arrived. However, the state of Texas seems to have forgotten about the Shonts brothers in general and Tom Mix in particular. With regards to the incident, former Governor John Connally (now Secretary of the Treasury) wrote, "Tom Mix was never employed as a Texas Ranger, in fact, he was never a resident of the State of Texas. It is my information, however, that he did hold an Honorary Ranger Commission that was given to him by Governor James V. Allred."[2]

Stories crediting Tom with being a former deputy United States Marshal are equally puzzling. Tom was billed as a former deputy

2. James V. Allred was Governor from 1935–1939. No documentary evidence can be found for a Texas Ranger Certificate issued during this time period.

Tom and Tony clear a gate. (Courtesy Tom Mix Museum)

"Pardon my intrusion, gents!" (Courtesy Tom Mix Museum)

United States Marshal in the picture *Ranch Life in the Great South-west,* which was released by Selig in 1910. With regards to Tom's service as a deputy United States Marshal, Archivist Robert H. Bahmer replied, "An examination of the pertinent records in the

"Let's not fight it, Tony—this train ain't ever going to stop!" (Courtesy Tom Mix Museum)

National Archives has revealed no reference to any service by Tom Mix as a deputy United States Marshal, in Oklahoma or elsewhere. The chief records examined were the records of the Department of Justice that relate to the services of deputy United States Marshals in the Eastern District of Oklahoma, 1908–1921; Oklahoma Territory, 1896–1907; Colorado, 1896–1912; the various districts of

I still can't believe it, but the caption is supposed to read, "Tom and Tony leap the old wagon cut at Newhall, Calif." (Courtesy Tom Mix Museum)

Indian Territory, 1896–1907; Kansas, 1896–1912; Wyoming, 1896–1912; and New Mexico, 1896–1912. These are the areas in which persons who previously have written to us about Tom Mix, indicated that he had been or may have been a deputy United States Marshal." Again, documentary evidence would seem to indicate that Tom Mix was not a deputy United States Marshal.[3] This letter does not rule out the possibility that Tom may have been deputized by a United States Marshal to help clean up a gang of local outlaws in Oklahoma or elsewhere.

Documentary evidence does exist to show that Tom Mix was a deputy sheriff and night marshal in Dewey, Oklahoma, in Washington County. Shortly after Tom and Olive made Dewey their home, Tom became friends with Mayor Earl Woodard. The Mayor asked Tom if he would accept a position as night marshal. Dewey was always quiet and peaceful during the day, but at night the gamblers and bootleggers were a problem. Since Tom had no immediate commitments at this time, he accepted a deputy sheriff's commission under Sheriff John Jordan, the Cherokee Lawman. Sheriff Jordan had a son, Sid, who was also a deputy sheriff. Sid was a first rate cowhand who had worked with his father for a number of years as a law enforcement officer.

Tom's duties as a night marshal were to curb the cheating and gambling by local and traveling cardmen. Instead of outlawing gambling in the town, Tom legalized it. He insisted that the gambling games be run by "honest" men and he proposed that fines, collected for cheating, be used to help build and maintain the town.

The scope and extent of Tom's work in helping to clamp down on bootleggers is best described in the following story. The story appears to have been written in 1920, shortly after the amendment on prohibition was adopted. The Fox Film Studios used the story as publicity for Tom Mix films such as *The Coming of the Law.*

FE-FI-FO-FUM! I SMELL SMUGGLED RUM
by TOM MIX

Every time I think of prohibition, I feel like a man who is living in the past. Having subscribed to a reserved seat on the water-wagon myself, I have no personal grudge against the constitutional amendment. But, I don't believe in coercing others.

3. A deputy U.S. Marshal Certificate, probably honorary in nature, was issued to Tom on March 15, 1934, by J. R. Wright.

"Whoa, darn horses, whoa!" (Courtesy Tom Mix Museum)

But I can't help laughing. I start thinking of the wily old foxes who will make life miserable for the law enforcement officers. No matter how watchful these officers may be, some folks are going to keep secret meetings with old John Barleycorn. The constitutional amendment won't make the slightest difference in their habits, except that they will work in the dark. The amendment has forbidden old John Barleycorn to remain in the country. Well, the lovers of the bottle will hide him, even if this means playing dozens of tricks on the enforcement officers.

I know what I'm talking about. I was an enforcement officer myself once upon a time. Whew, it was a hard job! It was a great job too, because it meant being alert all of the time. I tell you the bootleggers led me a fine chase in those early days in Dewey, Oklahoma.

You know, when that roaring western country became a state, liquor was barred.[4] It was up to me, the law enforcement officer, to

4. Oklahoma became the 46th state on November 16, 1907.

help bar it. I think I did help some; but it also required the help of plenty of six-shooters and nerve. The schemes that were tried in Oklahoma were many and varied.

Railroad trains, naturally, were ideal hiding places for the demon rum. We used to hold up the trains regularly to find out if there was any booze aboard. So expert did we become in detecting the presence of anything stronger than water that we could walk through a car and learn whether any bottles were concealed in grips, merely by kicking them. You know how a fellow can feel a letter and tell you whether it contains a greenback? Well, that's how expert we became in sighting bottles through leather and carpet bags.

Often the fellows tried to bring the stuff in small casks concealed in trunks. They soon stopped that, because all we had to do was turn a trunk over quickly and then put an ear to it. Oh boys!, we knew the sound of trickling liquor hundreds of feet away. Its gurgling warble is unmistakable!

It is easy enough to tell by a man's face whether he has liquor inside of him. But, I learned the art of telling by a man's face whether he had liquor on him or was more remotely connected with liquor in the baggage car. It's a great sport, finding a "liquor conscience" reflected in a "liquor face."

Another stunt they used to try on trains was to have a couple of bottles in grips. They would come into a car and say to some poor innocent looking duffer, or some sweet-faced old woman: "May I leave my bag here for a moment?" Then, they would disappear until it was time for them to leave the train. But even that did not work because the person with whom the bag was left disclaimed it the moment the officer asked about it.

We also kept an eagle eye on the trunks that were sent to Dewey. The most innocent looking wardrobe trunk, belonging to the leading lady of the circus, was examined. Many is the time such innocent looking trunks, when tipped over, revealed the presence of liquor. What did we do with those trunks? We cut a hole in the side, allowed the liquor to flow out of the opening, and then let the trunk travel on to its destination.

I had so many odd ways of detecting booze that for a time in Dewey they called me "Pussyfoot Mix."

You can imagine the ingenious stunts that will be practiced under the nation-wide prohibition law. Finally, of course, it will be enforced, but not before the wily old foxes have had their fling at foiling prohibition.

Tom's article, *Fe-Fi-Fo-Fum! I Smell Smuggled Rum*, is humorous and to the point. The fact of the matter is that prohibition didn't work. And for a time the bootleggers did lead the law enforcement officers a merry chase. Tom may not have been a law enforcement officer very long, but he certainly seemed to enjoy his work.

Sid Jordan and Tom Mix, ex-deputy sheriffs from Dewey, Oklahoma, became trusting friends, whose friendship lasted for the greater part of their remaining lives. Sid was a cowpuncher who was born in Muskogee, Oklahoma and educated at the Vanita, Oklahoma Indian School. Sid and Tom both worked for the 101 Ranch and Sid joined Tom when he started making pictures for Selig.

In 1913, Tom signed a new contract with Selig and moved his family to a ranch near Prescott, Arizona. Sid, who had tired of his job as a law enforcement officer, headed to San Francisco to catch a boat to South Africa. Sid had signed on to work for the Cudahy Meat Company. Sid missed his boat and found out that he would have to wait three weeks for another one. While he was waiting, Sid decided to visit Tom and Olive in Prescott. Tom talked Sid

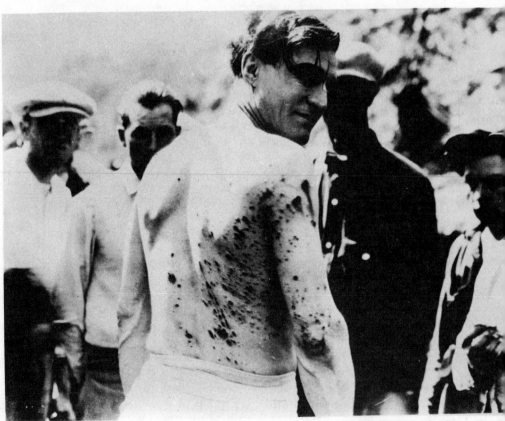

Tom's back was badly torn by a premature dynamite explosion during the filming of a Wm. Fox feature. (Courtesy Tom Mix Museum)

*Tom Mix and Sid Jordan clowning around with home-made chariots.
(Courtesy Tom Mix Museum)*

into joining him and working for Selig and the two men worked together, in motion pictures, for the next fifteen years.

Tom Mix and Sid Jordan pioneered many of the early movie stunts. Sid became a familiar villain in Tom Mix movies and the two men shared many narrow escapes from death. On one occasion, Tom shot a hole in Sid's hat and the bullet passed so close to Sid's head that it pulled some of his hair through the exiting hole. On another occasion, Sid fired a 30–30 rifle bullet that passed through the knot in Tom's necktie. Early stunts, with live ammunition, eventually gave way to the familiar "blanks" of present day movies.

Sid and Tom worked together from 1913 until 1928. At one time, Sid was considered for a starring spot of his own, but Ken Maynard beat him out. Producer William F. Fox let Maynard go after only three years and Sid continued on as an actor and livestock foreman. Tom left Fox and Sid in 1928, when he went to work for the Film Booking Office. Sid continued on with Fox and supported Rex Bell, George O'Brien and others well into the sound era.

A question frequently asked is, "How many times was Tom Mix wounded in his job as a sheriff or law enforcement officer?" According to *The New York Times*, Tom Mix was critically wounded four times; and, at the time of his death, still had three slugs in him as mementoes of his law enforcement days.

A former circus aid of Tom's said, "One evening, Tom took off his shirt and showed me 21 different knife and bullet wounds where he had been hit in his job as sheriff. They were all in his upper torso and he explained in great detail how he acquired them.[5] Tom explained, that in his opinion, a bullet was more merciful than a knife—it was like a tiny hot wire searing the flesh."

Stories about Tom being wounded have undoubtedly been exaggerated by various publicity agents. In all probability, he was shot, accidentally or on purpose, a number of times. Many of the scars on his upper torso probably resulted from wounds inflicted during his career as a Wild West Show performer and motion picture star. Tom's back, for example, was badly torn up by a premature dynamite explosion during the filming of a William Fox film feature. In Tom's own book, entitled *Roping a Million*,[6] Tom claimed that he had made over 370 motion pictures and never used a double. As a result of doing his own "falls," he had to have over 150 stitches sewn into his hide, not to mention the 33 broken bones and cracked ribs he had suffered.

5. A fold out wall chart, showing Tom's wounds and describing how he had acquired them, was even published for Tom Mix movie and circus fans.

6. A *Photoplay Magazine* reprint.

5

The Miller Brothers' 101 Real Wild West Ranch and Real Wild West Show

The Miller Brothers' 101 Real Wild West Ranch and Real Wild West Shows played an important role in the life and career of Tom Mix. Tom worked at the 101 Ranch at various times from 1906 through 1911. During this period and later during the Selig era—1910–1917—an impressive list of western stars got their basic training at the 101 Ranch. Among the roster from this school of hard knocks were Will Rogers, Ken Maynard, Jack Webb, Tex Cooper and Tom Mix.

Tom Mix returned to the 101 Ranch Wild West Shows in the mid-twenties, where he frequently appeared as a guest of honor. Later, following the Great Depression, this former guest of honor fought a series of trying court battles with Colonel Zack Miller, the surviving member of the famed Miller brothers' trio. In the end, the numerous law suits and court trials proved to be harmful to both parties. It was during this period that Tom felt that a good many of his old friends were now "trying to stomp [his] guts out."

The following brief description and history of the 101 Ranch is presented to show how Tom's life was influenced by these factors. Most of the information presented has been supplied by Jack Cleo Baskin, former 101 Ranch mascot and Ponca City fire chief. Mr. Baskin is currently active in Real Estate in the Ponca City area.

Tex Cooper and Tom Mix as guests of the 101 Wild West Show, 1925.
(Courtesy Jack C. Baskin)

The Miller Brothers' 101 Ranch was a fantastic place at the turn
of the twentieth century. The 101 Ranch got its name from the old
Bar-O-Bar cattle brand. The fact that the ranch was over 101,000
acres in size was coincidental. In the early days, at the end of a
cattle drive, the cowboys would let off steam by staging various

Jack Baskin, little drummer boy for the Mulhall Wild West Show Band. Taken at National Editor's Convention, 1905. (Courtesy Jack C. Baskin)

sports events which were later used in rodeos. The 101 Wild West Shows developed as a natural sideline from the rodeo events, after the cattle business began to wane. The Wild West Shows were spectacular affairs. They were too large in scope to be housed in a three-ring-circus tent. Troops of cowboys and Indians, covered wagons, stage coaches, and just about everything imaginable were used in the shows. The shows were put on in open air arenas comparable in size to a modern football stadium. Grandstand seats were on one side of the arena and a row of tents, housing animals, actors, coaches, and other paraphernalia, were on the other side.

The Wild West Show might consist of an historic enactment, cowboy-Indian battle, horse-thief act, or buffalo hunt. Regular rodeo events such as bulldogging, bronc riding, and steer riding were also staged. At first the shows were put on to help stimulate the cattle business. Later, the shows became a big business in themselves. Buffalo were even kept on the famed 101 Ranch as an additional drawing card or advertisement for the ranch and nearby Ponca City, Oklahoma. When the Santa Fe passenger train was due to arrive, the cowboys at the ranch would herd the buffalo from their pastures to specially built pens near the tracks where the passengers from the train could stop to see what a real Wild West Ranch was like. The buffalo pens became a routine stop for the Santa Fe railroad line.

In 1905, the National Editor's Convention was held in Oklahoma City, Oklahoma. For the occasion, the 101 Wild West Show joined forces with the Colonel Zack Mulhall and Pawnee Bill Wild West Shows. The editors and their friends were entertained at an arena set up in the buffalo pasture on the 101 Ranch. Fifty-three trainloads of editors and their guests came to the show to swell attendance to 60,000.

One of the big stunts for the show was to be an authentic Indian buffalo hunt. To add to the excitement, Colonel Joe Miller arranged to have Chief Geronimo released from prison at nearby Fort Sill, Oklahoma. The Indian chief was supposed to shoot and kill a buffalo bull with a bow and arrow during the skit. He shot the buffalo with an arrow, but the buffalo wasn't killed and the enraged animal nearly knocked Geronimo off his horse. Geronimo drew his rifle from a saddle scabbard and shot the animal again. This time the frightened animal headed for the arena fence next to the grandstands. Stack Lee, the World's Champion Rifleman for the 101 Ranch, shot and killed the animal before it could get out of hand. Some of the more "savage" Indians ate the raw flesh of the dead animal. The remainder of the carcass was cooked and served in sandwiches to the editors later in the day. The Indians, however, had spoiled some of the editors' appetites.

Lucille Mulhall, champion cowgirl, with brothers Charlie and Logan.
(Courtesy Jack C. Baskin)

The Miller Brothers' 101 Wild West Show Comes to Decatur, Ill., 1913.
(Courtesy Circus World Museum, Baraboo, Wisc.)

Later, the Wild West Shows took to the road and toured the United States, Canada, and Mexico. Each Wild West Show had its own list of "world champions." Lucille Mulhall became the Champion Cowgirl for the Colonel Zack Mulhall Wild West Show. Bill Pickett, a Negro cowboy who invented the sport of bulldogging, became the Champion Bulldogger for the 101 Ranch Wild West Show. Bulldogging, as invented by Pickett, differed somewhat from the present-day rodeo event. The cowboy would ride after the steer, lean out of the saddle and grab the steer by the horns from behind, then, he would twist the steer's head around, trip the steer to throw it, and bite the animal's top lip to hold him in the thrown position. Using only his teeth, the cowboy had to hold the steer down for a prescribed period of time, say ten seconds. The biting and holding action, like that of a bulldog, led to the name of bulldogging.

By 1908, Tom Mix had improved his image as a cowboy and he was added to the list of 101 Ranch champions, as Champion All-Around Cowboy or King of the Cowboys.

During the 1910–1917 period, the 101 Ranch became the proving grounds for future motion picture stars. Colonel William N. Selig of the Selig Polyscope Company out of Chicago and other movie pioneers used the ranch as a western locale. Several films were produced on 101 Ranch property.

In the 1920s, the cowboys went modern. By that time, they were bulldogging steers from a speeding automobile. In 1928, George Miller Jr. decided that bulldogging a steer from an airplane would be a spectacular event. He rented a Curtiss-Jenny airplane from Jack Baskin and Ralph Cooley at nominal cost. Red Shannon, Ponca City's airport manager, was to be the pilot and stuntman, Buck Hoover of Hollywood, was to do the bulldogging. Buck was to descend from the airplane on a rope ladder and bulldog the steer when he got within the proper range. Ten thousand people were in the grandstands at the 101 Ranch for the big show. But, before the plane could level off for its final run, it went into a tailspin and fell to the ground. Luckily, both Hoover and Shannon came out of the wreck with only minor injuries. Before most of the show officials could get to the scene, souvenir hunters were already tearing the plane apart. George Miller Jr. paid Baskin and Cooley for the plane and remarked, "This is the first airplane that the 101 Ranch ever bought and none of us even got to go for a ride in her!"

Milt Hinkle, the South American Kid, another alumnus of the

Bill Pickett, the negro cowboy who invented the sport of Bulldogging. (Author's collection)

101 Ranch, says the same stunt was attempted again by the 101 gang in 1931 at an airport dedication in Nuevo Laredo, Mexico. This time Hoover refused to make the jump and the angry Mexican

Feeding Mob Like This Kept 101 Ranch Overhead High

101 Ranch overhead was too high for the wild west show to survive when The Great Depression struck. (Author's collection)

crowd began throwing pop bottles. Milt decided he would bulldog the steer and he and the pilot made several unsuccessful passes at the bull from an airplane, which was a duplicate of Lucky Lindy's *Spirit of St. Louis*. The airplane was flying too high and too fast for Milt to attempt the jump. The plane's wheel structure was also in the way. Finally, a temporary platform was made between the landing gears and Milt decided to go for broke. Milt left the platform, ten feet above the bull and fifty feet behind him. Milt's shoulder hit the bull, bowling it over with such an impact that it broke its neck! At the same time, Milt's leg hit the ground and jammed his hip up into his body! The pilot, seeing that all had not gone well, crash landed the plane into the field and the crowd went wild. Hinkle was the "hero of the day," but he had to be hospitalized as soon as he was rescued from the cheering crowd. Milt suffered a permanent hip injury.

Milt Hinkle and Bill Pickett typified the type of men who worked for the famed 101 Ranch. They loved the sheer thrill of adventure and the cheers of a roaring crowd. Perhaps they had more "guts" than brains, but they also had their share of good old honest courage.

Tom learned a lot through his experiences at the 101 Ranch. He learned that the real cowboys could spot a "dude" or "drugstore cowboy" a mile off, and that, if you wanted to be a part of the gang, you had to pitch into the work and earn their respect. There was always room at the 101 Ranch for a cowboy who could prove that he was a real man.

The Miller Brothers' Wild West Show began hearing the death-knell during the depression years of 1929 and 1930. Money became scarce and the crowds began to dwindle. There were just too many cowboys, Indians, and animals to feed. Operations were no longer profitable, and in a few short years, a part of our American way of life was dead!

6

Cowboy Turns Actor

Tom's first contact with a movie producer came in 1909, after he and Olive had signed on with Will A. Dickey's Circle D Ranch Wild West Show and Indian Congress. The Selig Polyscope Company wanted to film the cowboys and Sioux Indians in action, so that they could use the Wild West Show sequences in some of their films. Most of the cowboys, with the exception of Tom, were from Montana. Tom was hired primarily to handle show stock and "throw a rope" if an animal went berserk.

Because of Tom's outstanding ability and showmanship, he was soon given a regular spot in the Selig lineup, as a supporting actor. The Montana cowboys were a bit jealous of Tom because they weren't sure whether he was a real cowpuncher or just some smart "drugstore cowboy," who had learned to handle stock in the Chicago stockyards. According to Harvey Hazelleaf, who was also with the Dickey show at this time, "Tom use to chum around with some of our bunch, but you could never say that he believed in tooting his own horn. Ask him a question and he'd answer it honestly, but he wasn't much on volunteering information about his past."

Tom's first big break came in 1909, during the filming of *Ranch Life in the Great Southwest*. The film was shot in Oklahoma's Cherokee Territory near Dewey, Oklahoma. Tom was hired to handle the stock and act as safety man, but he asked Director Francis Boggs for a chance to be featured in the film. Boggs consented and Tom was featured in a "bronco busting" sequence.

TOM MIX
SELIG PLAYER

Tom was soon given a regular spot in the Selig line-up, as a supporting actor. (Courtesy Tom Mix Museum)

*Old Blue, Tom's first movie horse, was also superbly trained by Tom.
(Courtesy Tom Mix Museum)*

Ranch Life in the Great Southwest was released by Selig in 1910.
On the billing were Pat Long, Champion Steer Bulldogger; Charles
Fuqua and Johnny Mullens, Champion Ropers; Tom Mix, Ex-
Deputy United States Marshal and Bronco Expert; and Henry[1]
Grammar, World Champion Cowboy—throwing and tying a steer in
14½ seconds.[2] The movie was advertised as, "the greatest western
picture ever put before the public." The picture was probably one of
the first filmed sequences of rodeo events. It was definitely another
"first" for Selig, the pioneer movie producer.

The filming of *Ranch Life in the Great Southwest* marked the
end of Tom's career as a safety man and the start of his career as a
Selig regular. Tom was first featured as a regular in a two-reeler
entitled *The Range Rider*, which was filmed in Flemington, Missouri. After that, about half a dozen Selig shorts followed, including

1. He was mistakenly billed as "Harry."
2. Microfilmed ad in author's files.

Tom Mix, Selig star and lady's man. (Courtesy Circus World Museum, Baraboo, Wisc.)

Briton and Boer, Up San Juan Hill, and *An Indian Wife's Devotion,* which were filmed along the Des Plaines River near Chicago, and *The Millionaire Cowboy,* which was filmed on the shores of Lake Michigan. (The films made in 1909 and released in 1910.) During this period, all of the Circle D boys, including Tom, were under contract to Will A. Dickey, who in turn, was under contract to the Selig Polyscope Company. (The star system had not yet been established.)

Tom Mix signed his first contract with the Selig Polyscope Company in 1910. At first, Tom was a little wary of the movies. The money seemed to come too easily, and he felt that the Wild West Shows were doing more than the movies to keep alive the spirit of the "Old West." Later, Tom realized that the movies had a much greater potential than the Wild West Shows, and that more people could be reached through this medium.

Tom's early western films were typical of the Selig era. A handful of regular actors was employed, and the balance of the cast was made up of local cowhands, ranchers, and businessmen. Actors under contract were paid about $100 a week, and the local cowhands earned about $5.00 a day. Teenagers, who were used as extras and errand boys, worked less than eight hours a day and earned about $1.00 a day for their labors. These wages were better than most occupations paid in 1910 and 1911 and the work was varied and exciting. One dollar would buy a "heap of groceries" in those days. The movies also tended to stimulate the local economy since livestock and buggies were rented from local businessmen. For a really spectacular production, a whole herd of cattle and their drovers might be hired for the shooting of just one dramatic scene!

In the summers of 1910 and 1911, Tom made motion pictures in Canon City, Colorado. While in Canon City, the Selig Polyscope Company filmed an action-packed one- or two-reel film each week, from spring through fall. Most of the time, it took only four days to shoot a film, and the cast usually had the weekend off. Most of them went to church on Sunday. At first, the Selig troop was welcomed with opened arms by the local population. The stars were wined, dined, and taken on sightseeing trips up the Royal Gorge. Later, the natives matter-of-factly accepted the actors and their films. Bill Duncan was accepted as the top star of the Selig troop while they were in the Canon City area. Tom Mix, Joe Ryan, Myrtle Steadman, and Josephine West were the other Selig regulars.

Photographs, 1911 vintage, show Tom Mix stopping runaway team of actress Myrtle Steadman (top left), local rancher and actor E. C. "Woody" Higgins.(right) (All photos courtesy of Lonnie Higgins)

Typical herd of local cattle used in a Selig two-reeler. (Canon City, Colo.)

The Selig troop rented horses and other equipment from local citizens, such as Woody Higgins and Charles Canterbury Sr. At the time, 16-year-old Lonnie Higgins, Woody's son, frequently played the part of an Indian. Many a time he "bit the dust" by falling off a horse that was running at full gallop. No trick cameras or faked scenes were employed, because the limited shooting budget wouldn't permit it. If a scene called for a runaway team to be stopped, the horses were whipped and one of the actors rode after them and stopped them. Luckily for Lonnie, young bones heal fast. Lonnie, now 70, still rides the range and recalls of how it was in "the good old days."

Lonnie says that after a hot day on the range, the cowpokes would gather at Hell's Half Acre Saloon for a few short nips. This gave Tom the opportunity to display his skills as a marksman. The boys would place lemons in a row of empty shot glasses and take a bead on them. The cowpoke that missed had the honor of buying the drinks. Lonnie says his father, Woody, and Tom were great pals. Besides Hell's Half Acre Saloon, they frequently visited the old coal camps, near Prospect Heights, when they were out to have a good time. The social activity consisted of singing, drinking, dancing with the barflies, and "raising hell" in general. (Tom had not yet perfected his image as the good guy in the white hat.)

Friends of Tom also recalled the time that Tom's wife came after him because he had been out on the town long enough.[3] Tom's wife was supposedly a little quick-tempered. According to the story, Tom went into the Elks Club and ran upstairs to the meeting hall, with his wife close behind. While a doorman temporarily barred her way, Tom climbed out of a window and hid in the awning. When his wife was finally admitted to the hall, she searched some of the rooms for Tom, but could not find him. "He's in here somewhere and I'll wait for him," she is quoted as having said. Then she went downstairs and waited outside by the front door. According to the tale, another employee came on duty at the Elks Club, unrolled the awning, and Tom fell unceremoniously to the ground. Naturally, he landed right next to his wife, who was sitting there waiting for him!

The Canon City area was an excellent locale for filming pictures because it had lots of sunshine and plenty of beautiful mountain scenery. While in Canon City, Selig headquarters were in the 300 block of Main Streat. Inside shots were made there, and the old fairgrounds on North 9th Street served as an excellent outdoors location. Other outdoor scenes were shot at the Royal Gorge and near the Hot Springs Hotel scenic areas.

Tom evidently did not renew his contract with Selig for the 1912 season. Instead, he went with Guy Weadick to Calgary, Alberta, Canada in March 1912. A history of the Calgary Stampede explains their visit as follows.[4] In March 1912, Guy Weadick went to Calgary to promote the first Calgary Stampede. Tom Mix made the trip west with Weadick to fill in time before opening with a new Wild West Show that Fred T. Cummins was launching in April for a tour of the United States. Weadick helped Mix obtain the position of arena director for the new Cummins show. Tom stayed in Calgary for a few days and then left for Minneapolis to visit friends.

Guy Weadick is generally given credit as being the originator of the Calgary Stampede. Little mention is ever made of Tom Mix. It is curious however, that two early news clippings have a completely different story to tell.

On March 25, 1912, *The Alberton*, in an article entitled *A Calgary Frontier Week is Proposed*, stated that, "The syndicate which

3. From *Canon City Record* obituary.
4. From *The Calgary Herald* of July 9, 1949.

is in Calgary promoting the affair is headed by Micks,[5] of Bliss, Oklahoma, who holds the world's record of 14 seconds for roping and tying a steer, and an Australian buckjumper named Frank Brown. They state that they can get 500 experts in Calgary to take part in the affair, which will become an annual national event that will mark the last stand of the picturesque western cowboy on the outer edge of civilization which is gradually, but surely, sounding the deathknell of the law of the Colts 45 and the rough and ready riders, who are now rarely seen or heard of, except in Russell pictures or western novels."

The second news article, published in the *Calgary News Telegram* on March 27, 1912, was entitled, *Cattle Barons Willing to Back Frontier Week in Calgary if the Cowboys Can Deliver the Goods.* An excerpt from this article stated that, "If the three Oklahoma cowboys, headed by Tom Mix, Champion Roper of the World, can show Col. Walker, George Lane, Pat Burns, Robert L. Shaw, M.L.A., and a number of oldtime cattlemen that they can deliver the goods and put on a Frontier Week in Calgary two weeks after the provincial fair, they will receive all the backing they want and be given 'carte blanche' to go ahead and make arrangements to bring to Calgary the best aggregation of ropers, riders, and general all round cowpunchers that has ever before gathered together on the American continent." The article then goes into greater detail describing the various meetings between Mix and local prospective sponsors.

It is interesting to note that these early newspaper writings make no mention of Guy Weadick's name.

While in the Calgary area, both Tom Mix and Guy Weadick worked for A. P. Day, a prominent rancher with a newly acquired string of bucking broncs. Day was interested in promoting the first Calgary Stampede and getting his stock in shape for the big event.[6] Day probably furnished the stock for Weadick's Wild West Show.

Shortly after Tom, Olive, and Weadick arrived in Canada, Tom wrote a letter to Joe Miller Jr., informing him that Guy Weadick was downgrading the 101 Ranch Wild West Show and trying to ruin its image in Canada.[7] Miller sent a copy of Tom's letter back to Weadick with a couple of his own stinging comments. Evidently,

---

5. Misspelled, should be Mix.

6. Based on information furnished by J. F. Day and the Medicine Hat Historical and Museum Foundation.

7. From the Glenbow-Alberta Institute files.

the letters didn't result in any serious repercussions, as Tom continued to star in the Weadick Wild West Show, which started in Calgary and ended in Montreal.[8]

Tom was seriously injured when the show was put on in Dominion Park, Montreal. During a bulldogging event, a steer turned abruptly and its horn caught Tom at the base of the jaw, knocking him unconscious and causing his jaw to bleed severely. Tom was carried from the arena and patched up. A few minutes later, he was back in the arena, insisting on taking part in the bronc busting event. He did, and this time he was thrown from the horse and knocked unconscious again!

The time was now growing near for Olive to have her first child, so she returned to her ranch in Dewey, Oklahoma. On July 13, 1912, Olive and Tom became the proud parents of a bouncing baby girl. Tom returned home from Montreal three days later.

For the balance of the 1912 season, Tom worked at a number of odd jobs, and then, in 1913, he signed a new contract with the Selig Polyscope Company and moved his family to Prescott, Arizona. Selig furnished a comfortable ranch home for the actor and his family, while they were filming pictures in the Arizona locale. Tom was also able to take a little time off to participate in the Prescott "Frontier Days" celebration. The following information is recorded in the July 6, 1913, issue of the *Prescott Miner Journal*.

"July 4, 1913—First day of the celebration. July 5, 1913—The Grand Entry on the field of sports was headed by Mr. and Mrs. Thomas Mix, of the Selig Polyscope Company. 1st Event—*Cowboy Trick and Fancy Roping*—Harry Knight proved victor over Tom Mix. *Steer Bulldogging*—Harry Knight—12½ seconds, Tom Mix—18½ seconds. *Steer Riding*—Tom Mix first, Nip Van second. July 6, 1913—Potato sack race won by Tom Mix, Captain. His team included Nip Van, Nick Frick, and Harry Loverin. *Cowgirl Pony Race*—Mrs. Tom Mix put on an exceptionally pretty stunt in the Cowgirl Race, in which Mrs. Henry Ritter outdistanced her by about twenty feet. It was a quarter-mile dash. Time—30 seconds. *Bulldogging*—All entrants of the previous day entered. Won by Tom Mix—16½ seconds. Harry Loverin, 2nd—20½ seconds."

The *Prescott Miner Journal* provides mute testimony to the fact that Tom was indeed skilled in cowboy sports and rodeo events. This was not true of most of the western stars who followed after him. The rodeo information presented above was the first ever

8. See *The Fabulous Tom Mix*, by Olive Stokes Mix.

recorded in the Prescott, Arizona, area. Since then, these "Frontier Days" celebrations have grown to become a major annual tourist attraction.

Later in 1913, Selig moved his main headquarters from Chicago to Hollywood. There, Tom became a business partner with Selig and was given his own studio and camera crew.

Contrary to popular belief, Selig produced movies other than westerns and Tom Mix was not his first big star. In 1908, Kathlyn Williams and Harold Lockwood starred in *Harbor Island*. A particularly big production for Selig in 1910 was *Wizard of Oz*. *The Fire Chief's Daughter* (1910) also starred Kathlyn Williams. *Back to the Primitive* (1911) starred Kathlyn Williams, Charles Clary, and Tom Mix. In this jungle picture, filmed in Florida, Tom wore the typical garb of the "white hunter" and braved all the dangers of a modern-day Tarzan. Tom is alleged to have saved Kathlyn Williams's life by barehandedly wrestling a leopard after it made an unscheduled attack on the actress. One of Selig's 1911 masterpieces was *The Two Orphans*, starring Kathlyn Williams, Lillian Leighton, and Fred Greenwood. *Cinderella*, also released in 1911, starred Winnifred Greenwood and Mabel Talifarrow. Pictures such as *Wizard of Oz* and *Cinderella* cost the pioneer movie producers a small fortune to produce. The purpose of these pictures was to show the public that classical epics could be produced and that motion pictures were truly a form of entertainment for the whole family. While the pioneer movie producers were blowing big money on the classical epics, the lowly one- and two-reel western films were gaining in popularity by leaps and bounds.

Many of Tom's early films for Selig were not entirely western. Some were pure comedy with a western setting and a few, like *Moving Picture Cowboy*, were actually comedies about making films. Most of the comedies of this period were directed toward an adult audience—the youthful audience became the target of a later era.

Tom's leading ladies under Selig were Kathlyn Williams, Myrtle Steadman, Bessie Eyton, and Victoria Forde. Although relatively unknown at this time, greater fame came to these actresses in the 1920s.

In 1913, Selig's list of stars also included Mabel Van Buren, William Stowell, Harold Lockwood, Charles Clary, Bill Duncan, Adle Lane, Wheeler Oakman, William Carpenter, Lafayette McKee, Tom Santshi, and Goldie Caldwell.

On December 29, 1913, Selig released the first filmed serial, entitled *The Adventures of Kathlyn;* it starred Kathlyn Williams (heroine), Tom Santshi (hero), and Charles Clary (villain). Fifteen episodes were filmed, and they were shown at two-week intervals. For some unknown reason, Selig didn't continue the series. The following year, the Pathé Film Studios jumped on the bandwagon and released the *Perils of Pauline,* which became the most famous of all filmed serials.

In 1914, the Colorado Motion Picture Company was formed. This venture was backed by Canon City and Denver investors. The Colorado Motion Picture Company tried to get Tom Mix to come back to the Canon City area and appear as their top star. But by that time Tom had risen to fame as the top western star for Selig, and the Colorado Company couldn't afford to match his salary.

J. P. Donahoo, a former Canon City Chief of Police, became the leading man for the Colorado Motion Picture Company. Miss Grace McCue was the leading lady and Owen Carter was the head cameraman. Carter stayed in Canon City after the rest of the Selig troop left.

The end of the Colorado Motion Picture Company came about as the result of a tragic accident during the filming of one of their pictures on the Arkansas River. During an attempt to cross the river, Miss McCue's horse stumbled and she fell and was swept downstream by the swift current. Carter attempted to save Miss McCue, and in the struggle both were drowned. Miss McCue's family sued the Colorado Motion Picture Company and won a court judgment.

Tom's Selig films are said to have improved in quality with the passing of time. Typical of Tom's later Selig films was *Along the Border.* This movie was written and produced by Tom and released by the General Film Service on April 8, 1916. Tom Mix, Victoria Forde, Sid Jordan, Joe Ryan, and Joe Simkins made up the cast of characters. A review of the movie stated that, "The story is particularly timely because of recent depredations of Mexican bandits on the U.S.-Mexican border. In the story, Grace, a rancher's daughter, and Tom Martin are in love. Buck Miller is the disappointed rival in love. Buck swears to be revenged and plans with Delgado, a Mexican outlaw, to capture Grace and her father and hold them for ransom. Grace makes a sensational escape and tells Tom and his pals of the outlaws' actions. Tom and the boys rescue Grace's father and capture Delgado and his outlaw band. The action is hot

Scenes from silent flick, Local Color *(1916) Girl from east arrives in west to write a story about the local color. Tom decides to make her stay worthwhile and poses as a tough guy. Girl interviews tough hombre. (Author's collection)*

and heavy and Tom gets his chance to perform many of his sensational and death-defying feats."

It should be noted that the cast of *Along the Border* was relatively small, the plot fairly simple, and the picture probably quite exciting and yet economical to produce. The movie is an excellent example of early films, where the star was also the chief writer and producer.

Tom's screen personality was well established by this time and he definitely wanted his pictures to be accepted as a form of proper family entertainment. He was proud of the fact that any mother could take her child to see a Tom Mix movie. He boasted that he never drank or smoked while on the screen. Tom was always the good guy—never the neurotic anti-hero torn between good and evil. Tom usually helped a girl in distress and won her heart in the end. Tom didn't really prefer to kiss the horse instead of the girl! Occasionally, the movie ended with Tom kissing the girl, but more often, they merely held hands and smiled affectionately at each other. Tom was rough on villains, although he seldom killed one in a movie. He roped plenty of them and defeated many in a good

Scenes from Local Color *(cont.) Mix shoots one of them writer fellers.
Faints when his faked wedding to the girl turns out to be the real
thing. Decides being married ain't so bad after all. (Author's collection)*

old-fashioned fist fight. He would of course use his gun to blast
the villain's gun out of his hands. Sometimes Tom would put on
such a display of expert marksmanship that the villains would
decide to completely give up the idea of gunplay. Why not surrender peacefully when faced with such overwhelming odds?

Tom's athletic skills and agility were frequently demonstrated in
his Selig films. He could mount a horse, lasso a villain, or jump a
fence almost faster than the old motion picture cameras could
keep up with him. Tom's films were often quite humorous—he never
lost his boyish sense of humor and the devilishness just naturally
seemed to come out in his films. In one scene, he emptied his six
guns into a stuffed dummy to demonstrate to a city girl from the
East just how tough an "hombre" he really was. Naturally, the poor
girl fainted as Tom pulled the dummy from a galloping horse and
proceeded to fill it full of lead. In another scene, Tom fainted after
he found out that a wedding he had staged turned out to be the
real thing.

In 1917, the Selig Polyscope Company ran into financial problems and had to disband. Most of Selig's stars readily found employment with other film companies. Tom Mix and Victoria Forde

Tom would put on such a display of marksmanship that the villains would give up all ideas of gunplay. (Author's collection)

went to work for William Fox, founder of Twentieth Century-Fox. By 1917, Tom was a well-known western star. Perhaps he was even more or less married to the movie industry and overly concerned about his public image. Somehow, his dreams of settling down on an Arizona ranch with his wife and little daughter had eluded him.

Old Blue was Tom's first range horse. (Author's collection)

Tom and Olive were divorced in 1917, and the following year he married Victoria Forde, who frequently starred as his leading lady, and who was a star in her own right. Tom and Victoria had something in common—their movie careers.

Perhaps the reason that Tom had so many wives is best explained by a former radio announcer and friend of Tom's. As he put it, "I always felt that Tom Mix and the other stars were victims of the times. Hollywood was pretty rugged in those early days—the jazz age, flapper era, etc. The film industry was comparatively new and so many were being swept into sudden success that it caught them unprepared. Most of them had not learned that there were physical limitations. They were still trying to keep up with their popularity and the demands of their fans."

Although Tom left Selig in 1917, many of his one- and two-reel films were reissued after this date. In some cases, features were made out of earlier short films by combining several reels. Two movies, *Twisted Trails* and *The Heart of Texas Ryan,* are examples of composite features which were shown in movie houses up to the end of the silent motion picture era. A review of *Twisted Trails* in *Moving Picture World* magazine gave the film the typical feature buildup: "Not only is *Twisted Trails* a feature drama in every detail; but there is some unusual photography contained therein, notably a rain storm, accompanied by vivid flashes of lightning, etc. Story from the pen of Edwin Ray Coffin, and is replete with exciting situations and dramatic climaxes." *Twisted Trails* starred Tom Mix, Bessie Eyton, Eugenie Besserer, Al Filson, and Will Machin.

7

The Big Times

It is not known for certain when the first western film was made, but *Cripple Creek Barroom*, filmed in 1898 by the Edison Company, is a likely candidate. The first "western" picture with a real story to tell was *The Great Train Robbery* (1903) which Edwin S. Porter wrote, directed, and filmed for Edison in New Jersey. G. M. Anderson, later known as "Broncho Billy" Anderson, played a minor role in *The Great Train Robbery,* and was the first actual western star. Anderson, an easterner, was rough and tough but not very glamorous. He made several hundred one- and two-reel films between 1905 and 1913; but before he could move into features, both William S. Hart and Tom Mix rose to prominence as western stars and beat him out.

Tom Mix started his climb to the top making early one- and two-reel films for Colonel William N. Selig. A few three- and four-reel features followed. When Tom and Tony joined Fox in 1917, both were seasoned performers. Tom had retired his first range pony and movie partner, Old Blue, in 1914 and purchased Tony from a friend named Pat Chrisman. It was still a little premature, however, to put Tony in the "wonder horse" category, or say that Tom had formulated the "costume" every western hero should wear. But by now, both man and horse were stars of feature length western films.

Tom Mix was a popular western star, but William S. Hart retained the crown of "King of the Cowboys" until 1920. Hart was a bug on realism—he looked western and he took great pains to make sure that

"Please lady, give me a lift." Scene from Prairie Trails. *(Author's Collection)*

his western films were believable and authentic. He rose to the top as a western star in 1915 and remained there until he was dethroned by Tom Mix.

Tom was not a western "purist." He did on the screen what he knew best how to do. He rode hard, performing daredevil stunts, calculated to keep the audience on the edge of their seats. Tony, who knew no other master than Tom, was superbly trained by him. Tony could untie his master's hands, perform amazing jumps, or pull Tom away from a blazing fire. And horses are usually deathly afraid of fire. Each stunt was performed with such perfection that horse and rider functioned as one. The lariat and six-guns added to the flashing adventures of the "Old West."

Tom and Tony executed nearly all of their own stunts until they became too valuable an asset of the Fox Studios. Even then, Tom would often insist on doing his own stunts and only permit a substitute to be used for Tony. Tom was the one who suffered when the timing of one of his stunts was slightly off. The close-up cameras usually revealed that Tom was the man fighting on the mountain top, riding his horse into the swirling waters as a bridge collapsed, and jumping from horse to train and back again. Possible broken arms and legs were the risks of the trade as far as Tom was concerned, and he paid the penalty more than once. Several times the shooting schedule of a Tom Mix picture was interrupted while Fox's top star lay in a hospital bed, recuperating from injuries received on location.

Above all, Tom Mix and Tony represented the finest showmanship of their time. The cowboy, in his broadbrimmed white Stetson hat,

"Glad I could be of some help." Scene from The Texan. *(Author's Collection)*

Sometimes a Mountie gets more than just "his man." Scene from Ace
High. *(Author's collection)*

Tom to the rescue. Scene from Mr. Logan, U.S.A. (Author's collection)

Tom strikes a pose with Indian children between scenes in Do and Dare. (Author's collection)

Camera crew getting ready to film another Tom Mix spectacular.
(Courtesy Tom Mix Museum)

and the well-groomed, white-stockinged chestnut horse rode together
to fame and fortune. The fancy duds and hand-carved boots were
never intended to represent the working clothes of the average cowboy—neither were the intricate stunts intended to represent the
everyday happenings in the life of a cowboy. The costume and
stunts exaggerated the adventure and romance of the "Old West"
and the audience loved every minute of it. A next-to-impossible
stunt was executed with such smoothness that it appeared as a
natural occurrence in a Tom Mix picture.

Selig never fully realized the great potential he had in Tom Mix.
He tended to keep Tom's salary down while at the same time making him completely responsible for his own pictures. Selig failed
to furnish Tom with any professional help as far as writing scripts

Tom's Beverly Hills mansion and swimming pool. (Courtesy Tom Mix Museum)

or devising plots were concerned. Some early writers have said that it is remarkable that Tom and Tony survived the Selig era. Tom was strictly on his own and he earned every penny he made under Selig. Tom learned the tricks of the trade through his own experiences and the quality of his pictures steadily improved despite these early handicaps.

Fox was quicker to recognize the potentials of Tom Mix and Tony. Fox used Tom's boyish nature to make a strong appeal to the youthful audience. Pictures such as *Cupid's Roundup, Six Shooter Andy,* and *Do and Dare* were specifically aimed at the younger set. Youngsters also frequently appeared in Tom's pictures and Tom always proved worthy of their trust and friendship. He was a first-class hero for any little boy or girl.

Tom could have been nominated for America's best dressed man in this attire. (Courtesy Tom Mix Museum)

By 1920, Colleen Moore had become one of Tom's leading ladies and Tom had replaced Hart as America's most popular western star. In the same year, Tom visited Jack Dempsey and engaged him in a friendly boxing workout. Boxing was a part of Tom's personal physical fitness program. It was also in 1920 that Tom's friend, Will

Rogers, appeared in his first movie, entitled *Laughing Billy Hyde*. Rogers became a popular motion picture star of the thirties, and in one picture Will did a satire on Tom Mix and western films. By 1921, Tom was one of the ten top box office attractions in the country. Other popular stars of the period were Douglas Fairbanks, Charlie Chaplin, Mary Pickford, Gloria Swanson, Lillian Gish, Richard Barthelmess, Constance Talmadge, to mention a few.

Tom Mix reached the height of his career with Fox in 1922. One milestone that year was the birth of his daughter, Thomasina, on February 12, 1922. Among others: His $250,000 Hollywood mansion was completed; his seven-car garage was filled with fancy imports; his salary with Fox was about $17,500 a week; he had bought a ranch in Arizona and the TM Bar brand was emblazoned on just

Tom boxed with Jack Dempsey, so Jack decided it was only fair play to swap around and ride with Mix. (Courtesy Tom Mix Museum)

Portrait of America's idol. (Courtesy Tom Mix Museum)

about everything in sight; he had a string of fine horses and a
large saddle collection—most of them silver studded; he had his
own permanent sets constructed at Mixville (also known as Tom
Mix Rancho) located on 60 acres in the Fox Hills between Holly-

No doubt about it—Tom was America's best dressed cowboy. (Courtesy Tom Mix Museum)

wood and Santa Monica; his initials were gaudily displayed in lights outside of his mansion so that there could be no mistake as to where Tom Mix lived.

Tom had an extensive wardrobe and gun collection. He had a roomful of boots and a white, western-cut dress suit. For special occasions, he had a purple tuxedo. He had a diamond-studded

Tony was a big star in his own right in the mid-twenties. He approves of the billing given to him on his special truck. (Courtesy Tom Mix Museum)

platinum belt buckle and diamond-studded spurs. His showmanship in real life was more flamboyant than it was on the screen. He dressed and acted as a top star was expected to by the public in the mid-twenties. Money was plentiful, times were good, and Hollywood gaiety flourished!

Despite the show of great wealth, Tom remained a real person. He was extravagant, but not snobbish. His old-time friends were still his friends and the money didn't seem to make any difference to him. In some cases, he was generous almost to the point of weakness. He would invest in a hare-brained business venture just to help out a friend. In many cases, he might as well have thrown the money down a drain.

Once, during a return visit to his old home town of DuBois, Tom told a friend that he would like to see another old buddy while he was in town. When his buddy heard that Tom was in town and wanted to see him, he remarked, "Well, Tom knows where I live." The word got back to Tom and he excused himself from his family and other friends and took off to look up his old buddy. Tom's buddy was impressed, a bit apologetic, and most happy to see that Tom hadn't changed a bit.

In 1924, Tom was sued by the 101 Wild West Show for breaking his contract with them. Tom's movie contract with Fox had expired, and at the time it appeared that he would have the 1924 season open. Tom signed an agreement with Fox to star in a series of westerns which were to begin in 1925. Thinking he was temporarily out of work, Tom signed on with the 101 Wild West Show for the 1924 season. In the meantime, Fox advanced the shooting schedules for the western pictures so that they were to begin work during the 1924 season. Tom had been more-or-less under con-

Tom was America's International Ambassador of Good Will. (Courtesy Tom Mix Museum)

Tom and Tony arrive in England (1925). Tony's feet are wrapped so that he could be exercised on deck. (Courtesy Tom Mix Museum)

Mix with mob of fans in England. (Courtesy Tom Mix Museum)

tinuous contract with Fox, and the movie industry paid triple what the 101 Wild West Show could afford to pay, so Tom returned to Fox. To settle the law suit, a compromise agreement was reached between Tom and Zack Miller in which Tom was to appear with the 101 Wild West Shows between pictures. Tom did appear with the 101 Wild West Show at Kansas City, Chicago, Cincinnati, Washington, and New York's Madison Square Garden. As it turned out, the publicity helped both Fox and the 101 Wild West Show.

In 1925, Tom and Tony visited Europe for the first time. Tony made headlines by walking up the gangplank with his master. Tom and Tony made personal appearances in England, France, Belgium, Holland, and Germany. Europe opened up her arms and greeted them enthusiastically wherever they went. They were welcomed

Tom had an eye for the pretty girls, and believe it or not these were the bathing beauties of his era. (Courtesy Tom Mix Museum)

Emmet Kelly, Tom Mix, and Ben Lyons—three favorites. (Courtesy Tom Mix Museum)

by thousands in every country; even European royalty extended their hospitality to Tom Mix and Tony.

Tom attended a Boy Scout Conclave in France and took part in Boy Scout ceremonies in Germany. Tom presented literally dozens of white Stetson hats, costing $125 apiece, to city officials, dignitaries, and deserving Boy Scouts.

Tom and Tony concluded their European tour with a personal tour of the United States and Canada. After arriving home safely on July 21, 1925, they visited Toronto, Boston, Washington, Buffalo, Detroit, St. Louis, and Denver. Then it was back to Hollywood, where their friends gave them a warm reception. While on his personal tour, Tom made it a point to visit Children's Hospitals, Disabled Veteran's Hospitals, and Boy Scout groups.

Tom was pleased that an American cowboy was so warmly received in Europe and happy that he was as popular as ever back home.

Tom's 14-year-old daughter, Ruth, entered motion pictures in 1927 and made a series of cowgirl films with Rex Bell. She was billed as a "chip off the old block," and Tom wasn't too happy about that. The "old block" still had a long way to go.

Tom made his last pictures for Fox in 1928. Shortly before the Great Depression struck, Tom found himself at odds with Fox policies, which he felt to be wasteful and extravagant. For all practical purposes, Tom himself had been largely responsible for the tremendous growth of the Fox Company. Because of the dispute and the fact that "talkies" were now coming in, Fox refused to renew Tom's contract. Earlier writers have said that Tom's voice didn't record well and that his dialog was unemotional and unconvincing. The fact of the matter is that Tom's voice was probably as good as many of the other cowboy stars of the time. Perhaps it would be more truthful to say that Tom was now 48 years old and that he found it hard to keep up with the pace of making a feature film in a month or less.

In 1928 and 1929, Tom made six additional silent pictures for the Film Booking Office (F. B. O.) which was then under the direction of Joseph P. Kennedy. Later, the F. B. O. film studios were reorganized as R. K. O. Tom's F. B. O. movies were poorly done and the film reviewers noted it. About *Outlawed*, the critics said, "Not so hot, Mr. Mix, not so hot. The saddle girths are slipping under the 'King of the Cowboys.' He'll do well to lay low, 'til he gets some new gags under his high hat. Here's the same old thing,

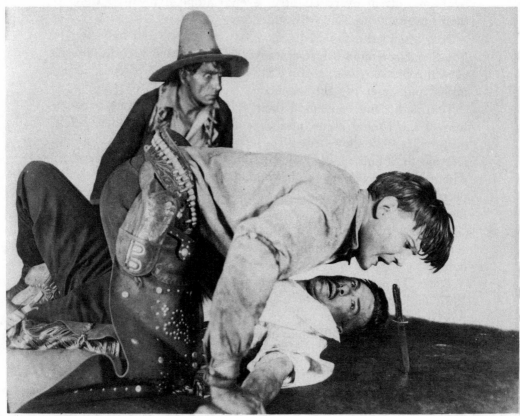

Buck Jones looked like Hart but fought like Mix. (Author's collection)

only worse, without enough sparks, color or action to keep an eight year old boy awake. Another flop like this and the kids will shout a lusty 'applesauce.' "

About *King Cowboy*, the reviewers were short and to the point with, "Please, Mr. Mix, don't do anything like this again." About *The Drifter*, reviewers said, "Tom Mix is bowing out. The jingle of his spurs will soon be an echo, the sight of his ten gallon hat just a memory. Vaudeville is calling him. He'll probably break little glass balls with a rifle. *The Drifter* in his cinema swan-song— his last picture on his last contract. Unfortunately, it won't emblazon the famous Mix initials in film history. Just another western, but send the kids anyway, just to see the aeroplane."

Other stars who suffered with Tom through the F. B. O. series were Sally Blaine, Barney Furey, Dorothy Dwan, Ernest Wilson,

Frank Austin, Joe Rickson, and Wynn Mace. Whether the pictures were as bad as the *Photoplay* reviews is a matter of opinion. It is doubtful that eight-year-old boys read the reviews before going to the movies to see their favorite cowboy star, but the reviews undoubtedly hurt Tom and his career. In spite of the reviews, hundreds of youngsters, including the Kennedy children, remained faithful friends and fans, right up to the bitter end of the series.

Like many others, Tom "lost his shirt" in the stock market crash of 1929. It is said that Tom lost about $1 million worth of stock, his Beverly Hills mansion, and his Arizona dream ranch. He temporarily retired from pictures—not to go into Vaudeville and break

Author's favorite picture of Tom Mix and Tony. (Courtesy Circus World Museum, Baraboo, Wisc.)

glass balls, but to appear as the top star of the Sells Floto Circus for three seasons. During this period, Tom bought Tony Jr. from a New York State florist and trained him as a performing circus horse. As a main attraction of the circus, Tom's salary reached a peak of about $20,000 a week.

Other people were also hard pressed during the depression years. One of these was Colonel Zack Miller, owner of the 101 Wild West Show. Zack's brother, Colonel Joe Miller, died after being overcome by fumes while working on his automobile. A year later, Zack's other brother, Colonel George Miller, was killed when his auto skidded on an ice-slick road near Ponca City, Oklahoma. The 101 Wild West Show was going bankrupt and Colonel Zack Miller decided to reopen his case against Tom Mix in the state of Pennsylvania. Zack resued Tom for $20,000. The case was resettled this time with Tom agreeing to pay $20,000 dollars worth of Colonel Zack Miller's past due notes. Tom was a pretty sharp businessman and, realizing that money was scarce, was able to pay off the past due notes at a rate of about 10 cents on the dollar. The reopened case against Tom ended, costing him about $2,000.

During Tom's eleven years with Fox, he made 78 top-ranking films. Movie titles and release dates are given in the Appendix.

Although a good many of Tom's pictures were made in Hollywood, Tom went on location whenever possible. He favored the national parks because of their splendid scenic beauty. He wanted everyone to have a chance to see a part of America the beautiful.

Whenever it came to filming a strictly dramatic picture, Tom seemed to fall a little short. It just wasn't in his nature to play the part of a stern, lone cowhand on the great prairie. Attempts to cast Tom in dramatic roles always ended with less favorable results than those roles which cast him as a happy-go-lucky cowboy with a virtuous lass to defend. Realism also knocked the props out from under Tom insofar as his showmanship abilities were concerned. The script of a dramatic western novel seldom left room for a departure to the daredevil stunts that Tom was noted for.

There were a number of western stars during the twenties. Among them were Art Acord, Bob Custer, Edmund Cobb, Ted Wells, Ken Maynard, Bob Steele, Tom Tyler, Fred Thompson, Pete Morrison, Harry Carey, Buck Jones, Hoot Gibson, and Jack Hoxie. None of these western stars ever equalled or surpassed Tom Mix in popularity. Of this group, only two patterned themselves after William S. Hart in any way. These were Harry Carey, who had a

Tom Mix and Victoria Forde enjoyed the big times together. (Courtesy Frankie Barr Caldwell)

relatively short western career, and Buck Jones, who only resembled Hart in appearance and dress. Jones was a fine actor and rider in the true Mix tradition. Jones was sometimes called Mix's top competitor in westerns. In reality, Jones and Mix were both Fox stars, and as such co-workers. The others more or less patterned themselves after Tom and were starred in so-called "streamlined" westerns.

Each western star had his good and bad points. Maynard dressed like Mix, but tended to go overboard on trick riding and elaborate stunting. Rooftop chases were a Maynard specialty. Gibson went overboard the other way—exaggerating the comic element in light western films. Pete Morrison wasn't a very good actor, but his films were noted for their exceptionally good plots. Jack Hoxie, with his horse and dog as his greatest assets, appealed to the younger generation. Perhaps the second most popular western star of the twenties was Fred Thompson. He was noted for his fine acrobatics, presented in a believable plot, and lively action sequences. Thompson's career ended with his untimely death in the late twenties.

Tom's rightly earned title of "King of the Cowboys" was never seriously threatened during the twenties. This in itself is a tribute to Tom, for he was then in his forties. He kept his body in excellent physical condition and he gave the rest of the boys a real run for their money. He exercised daily and seldom gained or lost more than a few pounds. Tony was a star in his own right, and Tom and Tony were a hard-to-beat pair in any respect.

Unfortunately for today's younger generation, few of the great Tom Mix western films have survived the ages. Many of the original 35mm negatives have been lost, damaged, or destroyed. In some cases, collectors may have the only 35mm negatives in existence and other negatives are probably dispersed and owned by a variety of organizations. Most of Tom's Fox films were destroyed by a disastrous fire in the Fox studios a number of years ago. Two films, which did survive, are *Sky High* (1921) and *Riders of the Purple Sage* (1925).

8

Publicity and Advertising

Movie publicity in the twenties, as now, fell more or less into two categories. First, there were the large movie posters made up of excellent artwork or a single large photograph. The posters usually carried the name of the producer, star, and film title—along with a simple "catch line" such as:

William Fox presents Tom Mix
in
The Coming of the Law
"in which a gun fighter is tamed and a woman won!"

Secondly, there were the press books and news releases. The Advance Notices, Tom Mix Shorts, Follow-Up Notices, and Press Books were used to advertise a particular picture. Their content was interesting, exciting, and adventuresome, but not always truthful.

A prepared advance notice might read as follows:

Tom Mix, the William Fox star, is coming to the Avondale Theater next Sunday in another western photoplay, *Fighting For Gold*, which is described as "rip-roaring"—in fact, a genuine Mix play. The story is based on the book "The Highgrader" by William Macleod Raine, and the scenario is by Charles Kenyon, the well-known screen writer and dramatist.

Fighting For Gold is said to be another splendid vehicle for Mix's daredevil stunts, with a pretty love story running through it and some good, hard, western fighting. A live bear is one of the big, amusing attractions. Mr. Mix has a new leading lady this time in Miss Teddy Sampson.

A typical last day notice for the same motion picture might read as follows:

Tom Mix will be seen at the Avondale Theater for the last time today in *Fighting For Gold*. Manager Ted Jones declares he would like to keep this picture longer because of the lively satisfaction it gave his patrons, but his schedule would not permit him to do so. Those who wish to be sure of seeing Mix in his latest startling stunts should go this afternoon, because the big crowds that have been turning out at night indicate a crush tonight for the last showing.

Now, who would want to be crushed in the big stampede to the theater on the last night? If the theater manager was lucky, he would have a crush that afternoon as well!

A suggested short for *Fighting for Gold* was the following story.

Tom Mix's Bear Rivals the Goat

A goat will eat almost anything. It does not hesitate to sample the inner tissues of a rag doll or the ball bearings of bicycles.

Bears are more fastidious in their tastes. But Tom Mix, the famous cowboy star, has a bear that must have had a goat for an ancestor— being the most promiscuous eater that Mix has ever seen. This bear devours potato peels and lemon skins with as much relish as he feasts on olives or honey.

In *Fighting For Gold*, Tom Mix's most recent photoplay, this bear had a part to enact. This consisted of rolling down a hill into the midst of a picnic party, and doing his duty by sandwiches and dainties spread out on the ground.

The grizzly rolled down the hill to perfection. But when it came to devouring sandwiches and cakes, the animal ate so fast that the cameraman got out of breath trying to keep time with him. The good food vanished so speedily that Director LeSaint feared the scene would be too short.

But bruin's goat ancestor came to the rescue. When the grizzly had licked the last speck of whipped cream off his nose and had made away with the last pickle, he attacked the pasteboard boxes that had contained the luncheon. Then he went for the paper napkins and paper plates; and was about to try his luck with the linen table cloth and silken cushions. But at this juncture Tom Mix appeared and, fearing for his pet's digestion, pulled the bear away.

Fighting For Gold is now showing at the Avondale Theater. It is a play in which fun and thrill are well divided.

A prepared short such as illustrated above would have certainly

"If I don't get ya, Blackie will!" (Author's collection)

gained the attention of any young adventuresome boy and a good many adults as well. Whether the details concerning the scene were true or not, you must agree that the news short was cleverly written and quite interesting.

"Catch Lines" and "Thrillers" were also a form of canned publicity available to potential advertisers. Examples of "Catch Lines" for *Fighting for Gold* follow:

"A rapid-fire drama of love and daring in the West."

"A tale of a miner who unearthed a heart of gold."

"A hurricane of action, adventure, and romance."

Examples of "Thrillers" for the same movie are:

"Tom Mix gallops down the road, overtakes the run-away, holds out his arms and catches the girl as she leaps from her seat to his horse."

"Tom Mix whisks out his gun and subdues lawless bandits in a barroom."

"Knives gleam, and pistol shots ring out. Tom Mix risks his life and saves the girl."

The story of the photoplay and its cast were also important advertising aids. In *Coming of the Law,* the cast of characters were:

> Kent Hollis: Tom Mix
> Big Bill Dunlavey: George Nicholis
> Nellie Hazelton: Brownie Vernon
> Judge Graney: Jack Curtis
> Neal Norton: Sid Jordan
> Potter: B. M. Turner
> Ten Spot: Charles LeMoyne
> Yuma Ed: Pat Chrisman
> Jiggs: Lewis Sargent
> Sheriff: Harry Dunkinson

The story of the photoplay read as follows:

Kent Hollis amazes Dry Bottom, New Mexico, as soon as he lands there. In the first place, his train fails to stop at the station, so Kent, by a fine piece of gymnastics, jumps off the rear end. He makes his way to the village. He sees a big ruffian insult pretty Nellie Hazelton, walks up to the man and smashes him on the jaw, knocking him flat. This man is Big Bill Dunlavey, the crooked boss of a lawless town, and no one ever before had raised a finger against him. A crony of Dunlavey, Yuma Ed, rushes to take Dunlavey's part, but Yuma Ed gets the same treatment.

Ignoring Dunlavey's threats, Kent goes to the office of Judge Graney—the only official in town who fights for law and order—and explains who he is. Kent's father had a ranch in Dry Bottom called the "Circle Bar" and a newspaper aptly called "The Kicker." When he died, Kent was an assistant editor of a newspaper in Denver. The father had fought for law and order, and Kent has come to continue his father's fight.

Kent divides his time between his two interests. He begins immediately to make the cowboys take notice. In the corral on the Circle

Bar Ranch, he does stunts that amaze them. He rides their worst horses, he even gets on the back of a wild steer and stays there. He learns so rapidly that even their bucking horses are under his control.

One day Kent is riding around the ranch and comes upon Dunlavey's men re-branding some of the cattle of the Circle Bar Ranch with the marking of the Circle Cross Ranch. The men see him and give him chase. As they are gaining on him he comes to a steep embankment, and down this, without hesitation, he rides his horse. The hill is so steep that even Dunlavey's gang refuse to follow him. They ride around in another direction and here again Kent pulls a stunt that sends them sprawling from their saddles. In one of the scenes, where the men fire at Kent, a bullet goes through the knot of Kent's tie. After Kent has upset his pursuers he gallops along until he comes to the home of Nellie Hazelton, where he tarries for some buttermilk.

Dunlavey goes to "The Kicker" office and offers to buy both the ranch and the newspaper. When Kent refuses, Big Bill tells him he will be run out of town. Kent laughs at this threat.

Big Bill sends a henchman, Ten Spot, to kill Kent. Ten Spot has always "got" the men Big Bill sent him to get. But in this instance, Kent takes the gun away from Ten Spot and gives him a good beating. Ten Spot, who admires the way he has been handled, goes to Big Bill and tells him he didn't shoot Kent and doesn't intend to.

Big Bill sees Kent riding out of town and decides to give him the beating of his life. He and his men ride after Kent; one of the men throws a lasso and pulls Kent from his horse, and they herd-ride him— that is, they drag him along the ground at the end of a rope between their galloping horses. Later they beat him unmercifully.

Hollis, in bad shape, makes his way to Nellie's cabin and convalesces there—the pair meanwhile falling in love.

Kent, knowing the sheriff is in Dunlavey's power, decides to run for sheriff himself; and on the morning of the election, being fully recovered, he goes to the election booth, disarms Big Bill and tells him the election is to proceed according to the law. Big Bill secretly sends Yuma Ed to Nellie's cabin, and when he finds that the election is going against him, he has one of his men tell Kent where Yuma Ed is and that he intends to kidnap Nellie. Kent hurries to Nellie's cabin. There is a terrific battle but Kent finally rescues Nellie. While Kent is away the better element in Dry Bottom decides to elect him and go to the election place and, led by Ten Spot, throw Big Bill out. Big Bill gathers a remnant of the gang and goes to get Kent. They meet him and the girl on the way to town, and give chase.

Kent has been elected, and a large deputation ride out to inform him of the fact. Big Bill and his gang get into a cabin and fire at the crowd from there. Finally, Kent gets an old wagon, fills it with brush, lights the brush and sends the wagon downhill. It crashes into the cabin and sets the building on fire, forcing the bad men into the open. Big Bill and some of his gang are killed, and the others are made prisoners. Kent rides back to Nellie and tells her that law and order have been established. She puts her hands in his. He takes her in his arms as the scene fades out.

From the story of the photoplay of *Coming of the Law,* it is easy to see why Tom's films were so popular. First of all, the story starts with a scene where Tom uses his athletic abilities to jump off a train that has failed to stop. Tom liked to work in train sequences in his pictures and he could easily dismount from a galloping horse while climbing aboard a train running at a comparable speed. Trains also provided an ideal setting for running gun battles between the "good guys" and "bad guys." Such scenes may now be rather commonplace in westerns, but it must be remembered that Tom himself pioneered and executed many of these early stunts for the very first time.

Next, Tom defends a fair young maiden from the clutches of a ruffian whose intentions certainly aren't honorable. Tom is alleged to have been as quick to respond to a call for help in his personal life as well. A fair fist fight, real or on film, was something that Tom just didn't back away from.

Tom then shows the Circle Bar ranch hands that daddy's boy can handle himself with the best, and in this way earns their respect. By this time, Tom had already earned several laurels in rodeo events, so riding another bronc or steer for the benefit of the motion picture cameras was no great feat. If an inexperienced "dude" would have attempted to do the same stunts, he probably would have broken his fool neck! The animals used in such scenes had to be high-spirited, or a few thousand movie fans would have demanded their money back. No one pays to see a fake cowboy ride a broken down steer—not even in the movies.

Next, Tom displays his skills as a fancy trick rider. He rides his horse down a steep embankment and circles around the "bad guys." Could he really ride a horse where other riders would fear to follow? Sure he could and so could you, if you'd been riding a horse and practicing stunts ever since you were a youngster. Then, Tom disarms a henchman and beats him, fair and square, in a good old fashioned fist fight. This was a tactic frequently used by Tom in his movies. No matter how impractical the situation might be in real life, Tom was aware of his youthful audience and he avoided a great deal of gunplay and violence. This didn't necessarily detract from the movie because the pace was fast and the adventure high.

Then, bad news for the hero. Tom is roped, pulled from his horse, and dragged about the rough ground. Now, nobody likes a scene like this, especially when it is followed by a good beating. The beating may have been faked, but the dragging wasn't. The closeup camera wouldn't permit even a good ringer to be substituted at this point.

Now the recuperation of the hero at the pretty girl's cabin can result in only two things. First of all they fall in love, and secondly it gives the kids a chance to go and get some popcorn while they are waiting for the day of reckoning to come.

Finally, the day of reckoning does come, and in a blaze of glory, Tom wins the election for sheriff, saves the kidnapped girl, and defeats (with a little help) a whole gang of outlaws.

When Tom starts his ride back to his girlfriend's cabin, the movie theater begins to empty and only the brave-hearted remain to see the two embrace and perhaps kiss. A former fan of Tom's says, "I can still quite vividly recall the breathless and intense interest in the action that held us kids spellbound during Tom's entire performance. It was only at the very end of his pictures—when he kissed the heroine—that any sighs of discontent would emanate from the youthful audience. Perhaps it was because that at that age, we could not tolerate any huggin' and kissin', but it was more likely that we had to face the awful fact that the picture was nearly over."

Another popular movie, *The Wilderness Trail*, reveals a different plot in a spectacularly different setting. The cast consisted of:

> Donald Mactavish: Tom Mix
> Jeanne Fitzpatrick: Colleen Moore
> Sergius: Sid Jordan
> Angus Fitzpatrick: Frank Clark
> Old Mary: Mrs. Warrenton
> Indian: Pat Chrisman
> Half-breed: Jack Nelson

The story of the play read as follows:

> The scene is laid in Canada, in the Hudson Bay region, a land of "measureless snows," rock-strewn barrens, and thick forests, a region where the law is a remote thing.
>
> The story involves the Hudson Bay Company, which has a territory as large as Europe, dotted by trading posts, and shows the life of fur

trappers of the north, among whom the "emotions are naked and primitive."

Donald Mactavish, son of Robert Mactavish, who is head commissioner of the Hudson Bay Company, has charge of one of the company's trading posts.

Old Angus Fitzpatrick, domineering, vindictive, jealous, cunning, head of the chief trading post, is Donald's superior, and as such, Donald is obliged to obey him by the rigorous discipline of the company.

Old Angus hates the elder Mactavish because, though they started life together, Mactavish has been promoted ahead of him. His hate turns against Donald, and so to hurt the father, he contrives to disgrace the son.

Donald is in love with Jeanne, daughter of Angus, but the old man forbids even friendship between them.

A quantity of rich furs have been stolen from Donald's district, and old Angus, seeing a chance to vent his jealousy, holds Donald responsible, tells him to recover the furs or be hanged as a thief.

To vindicate his honor and prove his innocence, young Mactavish goes alone on "the wilderness trail" to search for the furs, invading a region where the mercury goes 50 or 60 below zero and "life becomes something that is at best only mere existence and at worst annihilation."

He finds the furs, but is captured by the so-called Free Traders, men who hunt or trap without definite allegiance to any company—disposing of their catch to the best advantage; men who, in this case, work in defiance of the Hudson Bay Company and are eager to steal the latter's furs whenever possible.

At Fitzpatrick's post are an old squaw woman, Mary, and her half-breed son, Sergius, who is also in love with Jeanne. Ambitious for her son, the wily mother sends him to become head of the Free Traders, and she kidnaps Jeanne that he may have a pretty white wife.

By a marvelous stunt, Donald escapes from the thieves, and on his way back to take the news to old Fitzpatrick finds the stolen Jeanne in a deserted cabin, left there by Sergius in the custody of two men, one white, one Indian. This pair have become intoxicated and are disputing for possession of the girl. To save the honor, perhaps the life of the girl he loves, Donald attacks and kills the two desperate fellows.

Meanwhile the old squaw returns to Angus and inflames him with the lie that it was Donald who kidnapped Jeanne, and that Donald has joined the Free Traders.

Burning with rage, Angus starts for the Free Traders' camp, expecting to find Donald, and is wounded in a fight between his men and the thieves, and has his provisions stolen. He sends two men back over the long snow-bound trail to the post for more food. These men come across Jeanne and Donald, and offer them a horse that the distracted girl may go to her wounded father. Then, despite fiery old

Tom cooks a meal on The Wilderness Trail. *(Courtesy Tom Mix Museum)*

Fitzpatrick, Donald heads the party that captures the Free Traders' camp and recovers the furs.

Sergius, the chief thief, escapes and races away through the deep snow. Donald pursues and overtakes him, and there follows a fierce fight in the snow with knives, in which the half-breed is finally overcome, though Donald is badly wounded.

At last convinced of Donald's honor, old Angus relents and consents to his daughter's marriage.

The Wilderness Trail was popular because of its scenic beauty, its story of thwarted love, and its outdoor adventure. In the opening introduction, we have a common but unpopular situation involving employer-employee relations and Tom and his girl must innocently suffer for the hostility of their fathers.

Then, some furs are stolen by a gang of cutthroats and the action starts. The only part of the story that is a little hard to swallow is that Tom could be hanged as a thief, considering that his father is the "big gun" of the Hudson Bay Company. Nevertheless, Tom's honor is at stake and it is easy to see why he prefers to bring the outlaws to justice, rather than just "hanging around" or debating the matter.

The kidnapped girl, battles with the outlaws, and the relenting father are all elements of the story which in the end prove that truth and virtue will always overcome evil and injustice.

Thus far, we have seen examples of publicity and advertising that were typical of the mid-twenties when Tom was at the height of his career. One final example will show how producer William Fox made strong appeals, especially to the young.

Tom, Tony, and Constance Bennett—one of the more attractive publicity photos. (Courtesy Tom Mix Museum)

Frequently, the movie producer suggested that the exhibitors or theater owners should send a postcard or letter to Boy Scouts, Girl Scouts, and other civic groups. A typical letter follows:

To all Scouts:

Every Scout will see that in the following particulars, Tom Mix, the William Fox motion picture star, has the qualities every Scout emulates, and is worthy of recognition.

1. *Patriotism*—He was a United States soldier in Cuba, the Philippines, and in China.
2. *Courage*—He was an internal revenue officer in Tennessee, enforcement officer in Oklahoma, and a Texas Ranger, only because he was capable of utmost courage.
3. *Kindness to Animals*—His actor horses love him and he treats them with the greatest consideration.
4. *Personal Health*—He maintains a perfect physical condition by outdoor exercise and daily boxing with his trainer, Walter Williams.
5. *Cheerfulness*—Tom Mix never has a "grouch" among his company.
6. *Courtesy*—He never commands, he suggests, and his quiet dignity gets respect and willing cooperation.
7. *Honor*—Tom Mix was trusted by nation, state, and cities to clear Oklahoma and Tennessee of bootleggers and thieves.

The rest of the letter was a clear and simple plug to go see Tom Mix in *The Wilderness Trail*.

From the examples of publicity and advertising we have seen, producer William F. Fox must be given a tremendous amount of credit for promoting his stars and film productions, with an ingenious flare—he sold his work to both the theater owners and the general public alike, in a pleasing, interesting, and eye-catching manner.

The press agents of the Selig Polyscope Company, William F. Fox, and the Sells-Floto Circus made Tom a living legend in his own time!

The advertisements that brought moviegoers to the box office by the carload. (Author's collection)

FREE MATS—These cuts, except the large star cut, are reduced size (from 2-col. to 1-col. and from 1-col. to ½-col.). Mats of both 2-col. and 1-col. cuts free on application to any Fox branch office. Cuts at nominal prices. The same is true of art advertisements.

No. 1—One-Col.

TOM MIX
DIRECTION WILLIAM FOX

No. 2—Two-Columns

No. 3—One-Col.

No. 4—Two-Columns

No. 5—Two-Columns

No. 6—Two-Columns

WHICH

man will win?

A fight to the death is a big feature of the great photoplay

THE WILDERNESS TRAIL

a William Fox production
starring

TOM MIX

The man who never fakes in a stunt in his thrilling motion pictures : : : : : :

A wonderful story of life and love among trappers of the fur country : : : : : :

BLANK THEATRE

All Next Week

Ad. Illustration No. 1

Blank Theatre

MONDAY

WILLIAM FOX presents

TOM MIX

in

The Wilderness Trail

a stirring romance of the Northern snows

He puts a new thrill into the old struggle between love and duty. And he does it with a punch that reaches.

Directed by
Edward J. Le Saint

BLANK Theatre

MONDAY

Do you know this man?
Once Seen, He Never Can be Forgotten

If you haven't seen him
Don't Fail to See Him Now
He is

TOM MIX

He is to appear in a new and thrilling picture

The Wilderness Trail

A marvellous story of love and adventure in the fur trappers' land.

A William Fox production

Ad. Illustration No. 2

This is how one young couple in the old West did their courting. The position is novel, but they seem to like it.

The meeting was an informal one. She leaped into his arms to save her life — stayed there because it was comfortable.

TOM MIX

Noted cowboy film star does some wonderful Western stunts

See live wire "man who never fakes" win love and wealth

IN

"FIGHTING FOR GOLD"
A WILLIAM FOX Production
BLANK THEATRE—ALL NEXT WEEK

AD ILLUSTRATION NO. 2

BLANK THEATRE—MONDAY

WILLIAM FOX Presents

TOM MIX

IN

"Fighting for Gold"

A touch-and-go comedy depicting the perilous adventures of a dauntless lover in the West. Filled with virile action and lively romance.

See it and learn why Mix pampers the savage grizzly.

Directed by EDWARD J. LESAINT

His Pal Wears a Fur Coat

AD ILLUSTRATION NO. 3

9

CAUGHT ON THE JUMP!

A runaway team dash madly down a dangerous road, bearing in the wagon behind them a terror-stricken girl. An intrepid horseman, following to the rescue, comes abreast the team, and shouts a command. Only by a perilous leap from wagon into strong, waiting arms can the girl's life be saved. She takes the leap. Is it strange that romance was born in that embrace? The horseman is

Tom Mix in the WILLIAM FOX Production Fighting for Gold

A rapid-fire drama of the West   A play that grips the imagination

Scenario by Charles Kenyon   *Directed by Edward J. Le Saint*

BLANK THEATRE—All Next Week

AD ILLUSTRATION NO. 1

8

AD ILLUSTRATION NO. 1

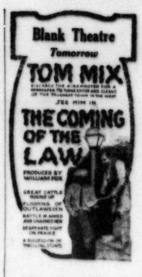

AD ILLUSTRATION NO. 2

AD ILLUSTRATION NO. 3

AD ILLUSTRATION NO. 4

7

9

The Sawdust Trail

The sawdust trail of the thirties turned out to be a rugged road for Tom Mix, the former William Fox star. His accumulated wealth of the twenties was gone and his movie future was uncertain to say the least. But Tom Mix seems to have had a remarkable ability to bounce right back after a serious personal defeat. After his F.B.O. film series disaster, Tom organized his own "Wild West" troop and appeared as a main attraction with the Sells-Floto Circus for the 1929–1931 seasons. In a way, Tom seems to have welcomed the chance to appear before live audiences again. Perhaps the applauding crowds and happy children helped to restore his faith in the future.

The Sells-Floto Circus employed 100 to 125 performers, with an additional 18 to 24 band members. Circus acts were called displays in the circus programs, and the displays featured performing mules, trick riders, acrobats, clowns, trained seals, dancing horses, aerialists, high-jumping horses, and other novelty acts. There were three rings and two stages, with something happening every moment. It was truly the "greatest show on earth!"

Tom usually led the circus procession to open the big top show; and after the regular circus performances, he and his troop of forty expert riders and ropers put on a "Wild West" exhibition for the delight of the audience. The circus Wild West Shows never failed to thrill the young and old alike and bring back memories of a bygone era. Tom was immensely popular with the younger generation, and frequently his admirers pressed so close into the arena

Tom as star of Sells Floto Circus, 1931. (Courtesy Circus World Museum, Baraboo, Wisc.)

that the show had to be stopped before Tom and his troop could continue with their "Wild West" presentation.

When asked by a circus aide why he joined the Sells-Floto Circus, Tom replied, "I started out on the sawdust trail[1] and it does something to you. It gets into your blood and now in these years, the old longing has returned and naturally, I returned to my first

1. Wild West Show circuit.

Tony comes to visit Tom, who is recovering from an illness. (Courtesy Tom Mix Museum)

Tom with his arm in a sling—one of his lesser problems. (Courtesy John M. Hall)

Tony Jr. does a camel-stretch for the cameraman. (Courtesy Circus World Museum, Baraboo, Wisc.)

love. This I enjoy and this I can do better now that I've had a great deal of experience."

But, the decade following the stock market crash presented many pitfalls, all of which took their toll on a man who, until this point, seemed to be filled with boundless energy and ambition. In the years that followed, Tom was plagued with illness, injury, marital problems, and numerous law suits.

In October 1929, Tom shattered his shoulder when his horse fell during a circus performance in Dallas. The shoulder had to be wired together. Several weeks later, it bothered him so badly that it had to be rewired. Tom put up with his bad shoulder until November 1930, when he had to be hospitalized because of back trouble. At that time, Dr. R. Nicholas Smith removed the wire from Tom's shoulder because it had led to arthritis of the back. Tom had suffered with a bad shoulder and back for over a year!

On March 5, 1930, Tom had to pay $175,000 in back taxes and penalties. Tom appeared in court in a brown dress suit and high-heeled boots. He carried his oversized Stetson hat in his hand and stood quietly while U.S. Attorney Samuel McNabb told the court that he had received the authority to allow Mix to plead guilty and receive a routine fine. Judge James fined Mix $1000 on each of three counts. During the court proceedings, it was explained that Mix's income statement had been prepared by Miss Marjorie Berger, an income tax expert. Mix claimed that he did not know how Miss Berger had handled his statement. Miss Berger was sentenced to a term in a woman's federal prison for the falsification.

In June 1930, Tom tried to prevent his 17-year-old daughter, Ruth Jane, from marrying Douglas Gilmore when they eloped to Yuma, Arizona. Tom sent a telegram to the sheriff in Yuma requesting that the marriage be stopped, but it arrived too late. When Ruth and Douglas were married, Tom cut off his daughter's $225 monthly allowance which he had been paying to her since 1917. However, Ruth sued her father for her rights to keep the allowance on the basis that he had agreed to promote her until she was 21 and a star in pictures. She stated that she had purchased a $13,000 home because she thought she could count on the allowance. Tom's lawyers contended that Ruth had lost her rights to the allowance when she eloped to Yuma. On July 5, the court ruled that Tom did not have to pay the allowance any longer. Ironically, Ruth's marriage to Douglas Gilmore ended in an annulment on July 9, 1932.

On November 26, 1930, Victoria Forde Mix obtained a legal separation from Tom on the grounds of mental cruelty and Tom's unexplained absences from home. According to the story, Tom frequently frightened Vicky by twirling a large loaded revolver on his finger. Tom filed a general denial of the charges but did not appear in court for the divorce proceedings, which were held on December 25, 1930.

In 1931, the Sells-Floto Circus traveled 14,891 miles, being on tour for 177 days, excluding Sundays. The circus opened in the Chicago Coliseum and toured St. Louis, Boston, San Francisco, Los Angeles, and other major cities. Later in the year, Tom was given an even chance for recovery from peritonitis, the result of a ruptured appendix.[2] A special serum was flown in by plane on No-

2. There were unconfirmed rumors that Tom was actually shot by one of his former wives.

Tom with diamond-studded platinum belt buckle. (Courtesy Circus World Museum, Baraboo, Wisc.)

vember 25, 1931, to save Tom's life. After recovering from the illness, Tom made a minor movie comeback, appearing in nine talking features for Universal Pictures. The titles and release dates are given in the Appendix.

The Universal pictures were popular and in the true Mix tradi-

No admission charge for orphans. (Courtesy Circus World Museum, Baraboo, Wisc.)

tion, but it was said that they were not enhanced by sound because of Tom's unconvincing dialog. Tony Jr., Tom's performing circus horse, made his movie debut in the Universal features. This time, the reviews were favorable—Tom had successfully avoided a second disastrous film flop!

In February 1932, Tom married Miss Mabel Ward, an aerial performer with the Sells-Floto Circus, and on August 18, 1932, Tom again went to court. This time the dispute concerned the custody of his 10-year-old daughter, Thomasina. A hearing was held on September 7, 1932, and newspapers on the 9th carried the following story.

A compromise satisfactory to Tom Mix, his divorced wife, and the judge today ended litigation in which the cowboy movie star had been attempting to win custody of 10 year old Thomasina Mix away from her mother. Superior Court Judge Ira Shinn approved a new agreement under which Mix secures the little girl's custody two months during summer holidays and on alternate holidays.

The mother, formerly Victoria Forde, Mix's cowgirl leading lady and now Mrs. Victoria DeAlazabel, wife of San Francisco's Argentine Consul, waived her desire to send the child to a convent for schooling and agreed to let little "Tommy" attend a Bay School, from which the child is to return each night to her mother.

Mix had objected to the child being kept away from relatives in any kind of permanent school.

Judge Shinn talked to Thomasina, with no one else present, and afterward said: "She is very fond of both her father and mother, both of whom stand before this court in an admirable light."

On October 22, 1932, Tom was injured when he was thrown from his horse, Tony, during the filming of a Universal film feature. The accident happened near Lone Pines in the Mojave Desert when Tony stumbled on a five-foot embankment, went over the bank sideways, and rolled over on his master. Tom was unconscious for some time and suffered an injured right leg and badly bruised side. In November, at the age of 23, Tony was retired to the Mix stables in Universal City. On Christmas day, 1932, after completing his work on *Rustler's Roundup*, Tom again retired from pictures.

Tom Mix retired from pictures, but he could not retire from the only way of life he knew. In 1934, Tom hired on with the Sam B. Dill Circus, a large motorized unit. The circus traveled about 14,000 miles in 1934 and made 222 stands. Mix acquired the circus for his own in 1935, at a cost of about $400,000, and took it out as the Tom Mix Circus. The Tom Mix Circus traveled 13,275 miles in 1935, 12,236 miles in 1936, and 10,521 miles in 1937. The circus made 216 stands in 1935, 217 stands in 1936, and 195 stands in 1937. By 1937, there were only 50 performers and 11 band members with the show. The Tom Mix Circus was also on the road in 1938, but it ran into financial difficulties and did not survive the season.

There are many reasons why the large motorized circuses ran into financial difficulties and were forced to close. Their fate closely paralleled that of the large touring Wild West Shows during the depression years. First of all, there were just too many hungry mouths to feed. Secondly, bad weather was always a problem. Cars and trucks bogged down and maintenance costs skyrocketed. To make matters worse, the crowds would not come out in poor weather.

Tom Mix Circus ads, 1938. (Courtesy Francis P. Clark)

There were other problems: diseases among animals, the injury or death of a performer, and looting and rioting in unfriendly towns. For example, Tom broke his leg on October 4, 1935, when his horse fell at a circus performance in Alva, Oklahoma, and on May 20, 1936, Tom's circus was flattened by a storm. Tom and three others were injured while attempting to evacuate animals. Such were the problems that at one time or another plagued the Tom Mix Circus.

Tom Mix in Mascot film serial, The Miracle Rider, *1935. (Courtesy Ray Beckner)*

Tex McLeod, Tom Mix, and Irma Ziegfeld—Majestic Hotel, Harrogate, Yorkshire, 1937. (Tom backed up one step so that he wouldn't look small compared to Tex. Note cigarette in Tom's right hand.) (Courtesy John M. Hall)

Tom tried to help "his people" whenever he could, but finally even he had to admit financial defeat.

One of Tom's circus aides said, "I only saw Tom angry once. His eyes became steel-like and seemed to turn to fire. He became tense and set and the real smart-alecks moved away from him by backing up." The incident happened at one of the sideshow attractions called the "Queen of the South Seas Isles." The attraction was staged in a 12-foot by 12-foot tent that had a canvas bottom about three feet above the ground level. In the rear of the tent was the living quarters for the queen, who was one inch under four feet in height and weighed about 75 pounds. The queen was very dark and was dressed in a beautiful scarlet gown with an intricate design. She sat in the middle of the canvas and handled all sorts of deadly snakes. She permitted the snakes to crawl all over her. There were usually about 80 snakes on the canvas with her. Most of the snakes were various types of rattlesnakes, with a few of the more exotic varieties thrown in to add to the attraction. A couple of snake handlers were in the process of carefully adding a newly caught rattler to the group when a couple of ruffians came up. They angered the rattlesnake with the handler's sticks and the snake struck at the queen, barely missing her. Tom rushed to the scene and said, "You two beat it, now!" Tom was angry and the two ruffians knew it. The ruffians didn't answer, they just backed away and high-tailed it out of there!

The "Queen of the South Seas Isles" was a typical sideshow attraction: the queen wasn't really a queen and she certainly wasn't from the South Seas Isles. In fact, she was really a small Black boy of undeterminable age!

Tom came out of movie retirement for a time in 1935 to film a serial entitled *The Miracle Rider* for Mascot Pictures. According to Tom, he returned to Hollywood to film the series because, "I was mad at the conditions I saw and read about every day. Criminals on the loose. Boys and girls learning Communist propaganda in the schools. Crime filling the newspapers. Finally, I figured out a way that I could help—by returning to the screen with a picture with some good old-fashioned virtues and justice."

Tom's comments are ironic in that the same cries are heard today in many places. Nevertheless, it is difficult to see how *The Miracle Rider* serial could have helped the situation, even if it did exist. But, as one reporter of the day put it, "Tom's one fellow who will never have to worry about being shot for being too modest!"

Tom and Tony II in Birmingham, England. This photo was taken in New Street Station prior to Tom's opening at the Birmingham Hippodrome. (Courtesy John M. Hall)

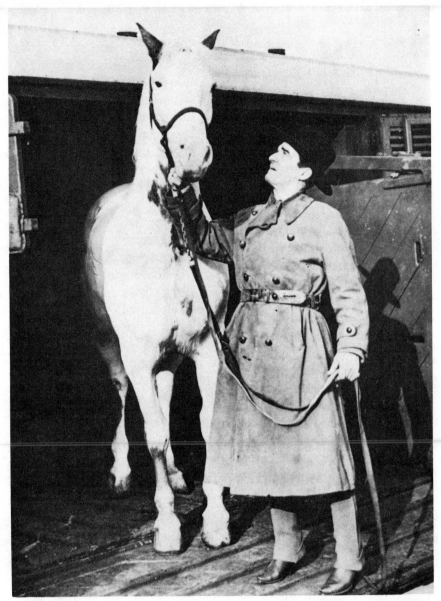

Tom arriving at Cardiff in Wales, 1938. (Tom used Tony II in England because he was such a large horse and all the English horses seemed big alongside of old Tony.) (Courtesy John M. Hall)

Tom seems to have made the complete circle in life from the time that "he didn't believe in tooting his own horn."[3]

The Miracle Rider consisted of 33 reels and was a novel story of

3. See *Cowboy Turns Actor*, page 74.

Tom on Tony II: Rotten Row, London, 1938. (Courtesy John M. Hall)

the modern west. Tom played the part of a Texas Ranger, who braved a thousand deaths to unravel a plot to force his Indian friends from their beloved reservation. Tony Jr. helped Tom display his famous riding tricks in the serial. The first episode consisted of five reels, with two reels in each of the remaining episodes. Episode titles are given in the Appendix.

Many writers have said that it might have been better if Tom had stayed retired from pictures. The Mascot series were crudely done, and had weak plots and poor filming techniques. Tom himself seemed to run out of steam after the first couple of episodes, and from that point on the series wasn't worth the time and effort he put into it. On the other hand, a new generation of youngsters did get to see Tom Mix in the movies, even if he wasn't at his best.

During the late thirties, Tom turned to drink to help drown his sorrows. On more than one occasion, he failed to make a personal appearance, mainly because he was "under the influence." His personal friends began to worry when Tom took off in the middle of the night, in his over-powered sports car, to "get away from it all." On one occasion, Tom slugged a spectator outside of his circus tent and was taken to court on an aggravated assault charge. Those who loved Tom hated to see him drinking to excess and they were

Tom and Tony II in London, 1938. (Courtesy John M. Hall)

reasonably successful in talking him into taking hold of his senses and returning to moderation.

On April 11, 1938, Tom Mix ended his 1933 contract with the Ralston Purina Company and signed a new contract to continue the youth oriented radio programs, which followed the filmed-serial style. Tom endorsed the Ralston Purina products as helping to build a better and stronger youth throughout America and the Ralston Company held the boys and girls spellbound for 15 minutes each day.

In May 1938 Tom left for a second European tour. He arrived in England on May 20th and the police promptly took eight pistols and five rifles away from Tom because he had no import license. One reporter wrote that Tom's arrival in England "must have been the largest armed force that has tried to land on British soil since the last attempt by the Stuarts, almost 200 years ago." In September, Tom and Tony II[4] were big hits at the Birmingham Hippodrome Theatre. Reviews of his performance noted Tom's unerring marksmanship in which "he splits a bullet on the edge of a butcher's cleaver, so that one bullet smashes two objects placed on either side of the cleaver."

After a second royal welcome, Tom returned to America with new hopes and ideas. He was convinced that he was still very popular and he felt that another movie comeback might not be impossible after all.

4. A white horse, not to be confused with Tony Jr.

10

The Riderless Pony

Tom's circus had folded for good, and he had moved his livestock to a little ranch about 20 miles from Hollywood. He had finished his second personal appearance tour of England and was making a series of appearances in this country.

However, death intervened, on a lonely highway, 18 miles from Florence, Arizona. The date was Saturday, October 12, 1940. At 2 P.M., Tom had made a personal appearance in Tucson, Arizona, and was headed for Phoenix, the next stop on his schedule. While in Tucson, Tom had visited with Sheriff Ed Echols, an old friend, and Walt Coburn, a writer. Tom also planned to stop off at Florence, Arizona, to visit with Harry Knight, a former rodeo champion, who had been married to his oldest daughter. Tom was alone in his green custom-built Cord roadster when he suddenly came upon a crew of highway workers. He swerved into a detour and the car went down a dry wash and up the other side where it overturned, pinning him beneath the wreckage. It is doubtful that Tom ever knew what hit him, or that he suffered any pain. A metal suitcase, on the back ledge of the car, was believed to have broken his neck on impact. He was dead when highway workers freed his broken body. His cream-colored western dress suit remained virtually unwrinkled.

According to various news releases, Tom died wearing his boots, diamond-studded belt buckle, and white 10-gallon Stetson hat. His pockets contained $6000 in cash and $1500 in traveler's checks.

Mrs. Mabel Ward Mix, Tom's last wife, and Mrs. Mary Stone, a friend, flew with stunt pilot Paul Mantz from Hollywood to Florence to claim the body. A small group of friends met the sleek red airplane on its return trip to the Union Air Terminal in Hollywood.

Most of Tom's friends and relatives were shocked at the news of his tragic ending. To some it was not a total shock or surprise, for he was known as a hard driver, just as he was a hard fighter and rider. In Hollywood, William S. Hart, one of Tom's good friends, said, "It's just too awful. My recollections of Tom are still very vivid. He was wonderful." Mary Pickford, a one-time neighbor of Tom, said, "I think he would have wanted it to come just as quickly as it did." In Madison Square Garden, Gene Autry paid tribute to Tom as being one of the leading promoters of cowboy sports.

Tom's friends agreed that Tom wanted to be remembered, first, last, and always, as a cowboy. He had lived up to what he thought a cowboy's image should be—he rode hard, fought hard, and used his six-guns, when necessary. He didn't believe in yodeling and guitar strummin'.

Tom's body was placed in the Pierce Brothers' Mortuary and his friends paid their last respects to him at the Little Church of Flowers. A Masonic Ritual was read by Monte Blue, a close personal friend, and Orchestra Leader Rudy Vallee sang Tom's favorite song, "Empty Saddles." Tom was buried in an extravagant silver casket, which bore the famous T.M. initials in block lettering. Funeral services were conducted by the Reverend J. Whitcomb Bougher and Tom was laid to rest in Glendale's Forest Lawn Memorial Park near the graves of Jean Harlow, Douglas Fairbanks, and Marie Dressler. Tom was buried with full military and Masonic honors.

During his lifetime, Tom had earned over $6 million. But in spite of his great show of wealth in the twenties, and the lavish funeral arrangements, at the time of his death Tom was reported to have left only a modest estate—worth about $115,000. According to the *South Bend Times*, Ralph Smith, Tom's attorney, estimated that the amount of the estate might even be cut in half by the time the obligations of the estate were discharged. The *Peru Daily Tribune* of October 19, 1940, revealed that according to the terms of Tom's will, four former wives and one daughter would be cut off without a penny. Tom's will, dated January 31, 1938, bequeathed the actor's entire estate to Mrs. Mabel Hubbell Mix, and one of his two daughters, Mrs. Thomasina Mix Matthews, age 19. A life long friend,

Riderless pony marks the spot of Mix's fatal accident. (Photo by Don Stillman)

Inscription on Arizona Highway Memorial. (Photo by Don Stillman)

Ivan D. Parker, received Tom's famous horse, Tony, and all of Tom's western regalia.

Some time after Tom's death, the Pinal County Historical Society of Florence, Arizona, erected a seven-foot-high statue of a riderless pony to mark the spot where Tom's fatal automobile accident occurred. The inscription on the monument, written by former Society President A. W. Gressinger, reads as follows:

Jan. 6, 1880–Oct. 12, 1940[1]
In memory of Tom Mix
whose spirit left his body on this spot
and whose characterizations and portrayals

1. On October 12, 1942, exactly two years after Tom's death, Tom's famed movie horse, old Tony, followed him in death.

> in life served to better fix memories of
> the old west in the minds of living men.

Needless to say, Tom's death did not put an end to his fame or legend. The Tom Mix Radio Show continued until 1950. Thousands of youngsters listened to the familiar Ralston Theme Song each day. In the radio show, Tom lived on the T Bar M Ranch in Dobie Township. His horse, Tony, frequently rescued Tom from outlaws. Tom's friends and cohorts were known as Straight-Shooters and one of the main points of the program was that Straight-Shooters always win! Sheriff Mike Shaw was Tom's sidekick who assisted him in rounding up the outlaws. (See the Appendix for program details.)

In 1947 and 1953, Fawcett Publications, Inc. and Charlton Comics issued a series of comic books featuring the adventures of Tom Mix. The comics were poorly done and highly fictional in nature. Only

Oil painting of Tom Mix at Tom Mix Museum. (Author's collection)

The author's son, Tom, on the Tom Mix Museum's replica of Tony. (Author's collection)

General view of the Tom Mix Museum. (Courtesy Tom Mix Museum)

a limited number were printed and they never really became popular. For these reasons, the comic books are now considered to be collector's items.

On June 30, 1966, a group of Washington County, Oklahoma, residents left for California to buy Tom's western regalia collection. The collection, once insured for $1 million, was purchased for $40,000 from Milton Uhler of Van Nuys, California. The memorabilia was left to Uhler by his late uncle, Ivan Parker. Parker had been written into Tom's will because he had taken care of old Tony, after the horse was retired. It was also rumored that Parker had helped Tom financially with his circus ventures. Tom's personal property had been put into storage for about 25 years prior to its purchase by the Oklahoma group.

The money to purchase Tom's collection was raised by the Dewey, Oklahoma, Jaycees in ten days. A non-profit civic corporation, known as the Tom Mix Museum, Inc., was then formed by Dewey and Bartlesville, Oklahoma, citizens. The real work began with the construction of a large block and brick museum building, two blocks west of Dewey's main intersection. Mr. Edgar Weston, the museum curator, went to work inside the building constructing glass showcases to display the collection. Members of the civic corporation picked up a 50-year-old horse mannequin from the Woolaroc Museum. Years ago, the mannequin had been used by a saddle shop to display goods. With considerable artistic talent, Mrs. Geraldine Weston began to reshape the mannequin into a likeness of old Tony. She added about 150 pounds of asbestos fibre, dry glue, pottery plaster and paint to the mannequin. The countless hours of work invested by Mrs. Weston were well worth the effort, however, for the Tom Mix Museum now proudly displays a full-size, life-like replica of Tony, the famed "wonder horse." A 25-foot-high sign was also erected in front of the building, just prior to the museum's grand opening.

The Tom Mix Museum had its grand opening on June 1, 1968. Tom's daughter, Ruth Mix Hill, and grandson Hickman Hill, took part in the ribbon cutting ceremony and Monty Montana, a former friend of Tom's, autographed hundreds of white souvenir hats bearing the famous T Bar M brand. Monty also starred in a western show which was held Saturday night at the Dewey Rodeo Arena. Despite threatening clouds, which had formed earlier in the day, the grand opening proved to be a great success.

Included in the museum collection are about 20 saddles, 15 pis-

Part of the famous Mix wardrobe collection, which is now on display at the Tom Mix Museum. (Author's collection)

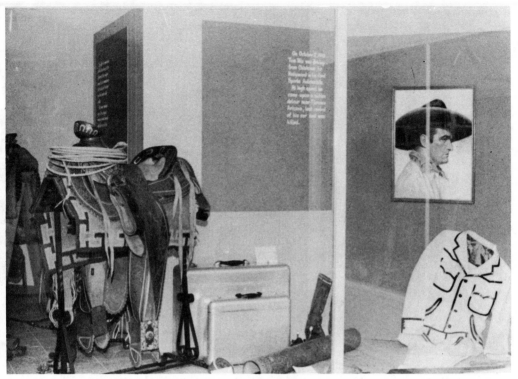

The suitcase responsible for Tom's death and part of the Tom Mix Museum Collection. (Author's collection)

tols, 18 rifles, 5000 photographs, Tom's honorable discharge, a Texas Ranger certificate, many of his motion picture and circus costumes, and the suitcase responsible for his death. Most of these items are now on display. In the future, the museum plans to expand its facilities so that all of the collection can be put on display. W. L. Halter, museum corporation president, has aspirations of someday adding Tom's Cord automobile to the collection. The death car has been restored and is still in operation in California.

In the late sixties, considerable interest was generated within the Pennsylvania Historical and Museum Commission toward the erection of a historical highway marker, near the birthplace of Tom Mix. Interest in this project was stimulated by persons seeking more information about Tom's boyhood and by general public acceptance of the fact that Tom Mix was actually born in Mix Run, Pennsylvania, and not El Paso, Texas, as formerly widely publicized. Outside interests in the project rekindled the spirits of local

Opening day of the Tom Mix Museum. Monty Montana at the rostrum with Tom's daughter, Ruth Mix Hill, at far right and grandson, Hickman Hill, third from right in front row. (Courtesy Tom Mix Museum)

members of the Cameron County[2] Historical Society, who followed the project to its logical conclusion.

Late in July 1968, the state historical commission completed the erection of the marker and the construction of a roadside pull-off, and on August 8, 1968, the marker was officially dedicated by the Cameron County Historical Society, with the traditional "breaking" of a champagne bottle.

The highway marker inscription, written by A. Henry Haas,[3] reads as follows:

Tom Mix

The famous cowboy star of silent
motion pictures was born a short
distance from here on January 6,
1880. He served as a soldier in

2. Mix Run county location.
3. The author assisted in preparing the text and dedicating the marker.

Pennsylvania highway marker inscription. (Author's collection)

The author with Mrs. Frankie Barr Caldwell at Marker Dedication. (Author's collection)

the Spanish-American War, later
becoming renowned for his "wild
west" roles in cinema and circus.
Mix died in an auto accident in
Arizona on October 12, 1940.

Following the marker dedication, a group of about 40 persons toured the old Mix homestead, and later in the evening the regular dinner meeting of the Cameron County Historical Society was held. Mr. John Nicholas, author of *Riding Up To Glory, The Life of Tom Mix,* was one of the guest speakers who spoke to a capacity crowd of about 80 persons.

The marker dedication was held during the week of the Cameron County Fair, and twice daily Tom Mix movies were shown in a tent on the fairgrounds. Businessmen at Emporium, the county seat, displayed Tom Mix memorabilia in local store windows and several local reporters covered the affair.

For those interested in visiting the Tom Mix historical marker, it is located on highway 555, just west of Driftwood, Pennsylvania. A roadside pull-off with picnic tables awaits the weary traveler in this scenic mountain area.

11

The Legend of Tom Mix

Most of the legendary tales about Tom Mix deal with his birth, boyhood, military service, experience as a law enforcement officer, and early motion picture work. All in all, these stories tended to create an image of Tom comparable with that of the Lone Ranger or Renfrew of the Mounties. The reason for the fabrication of these tales is obvious—they created an inspiring, exciting, adventuresome image of a heroic cowboy, something that would tend to lure the public into the old nickelodeon. Also, the stories nicely filled the less romantic gaps in Tom's life, such as when he was a bartender, drum major, inexperienced cowboy, etc.

Soon the legend grew to become a ten-headed dragon that was very difficult to slay without killing the man himself. Those who recognized the dragon for what it was kept mum. Why ruin a man's career for the sake of being precise? What the public really wanted was first-class entertainment at a reasonable price, and that's exactly what Tom Mix and the early movie producers gave them.

In retrospect, it looks like Tom probably didn't need his ten-headed friend to succeed. Surely, his personality and showmanship would have eventually carried him to the top. But once the legend was established there really wasn't much that he could do, except go along with the "super-sales" pitch.

The Sells-Floto Circus Program of 1931 carried the following story of Tom's life. It is a good summary of the legend planted by publicity agents, nourished by Tom's own acts, and left to grow in the minds and hearts of young and old.

In a small cabin, about forty miles north of El Paso, Texas, Tom Mix first saw the light of day. In that primitive dwelling, on January 6, 1880, the idol of young America, the beloved hero of the entire civilized world, emitted his first wild west whoop.

Tom is one-eighth Cherokee Indian—and proud of the fact. His great-grandfather, who lived in the White Eagle Reserve, first translated the Bible into the Osage language. His father, Captain Mix of the Seventh U. S. Cavalry, participated in the thrilling adventures of the early days in Texas and the border region before law and order were established.

Being a native-born son of the great southwest, it is not surprising that Tom was raised among its cattle and cowboys, that he lived their life and shared their difficulties and dangers, as well as their mirth and merrymaking. And that he too, was a pioneer of pioneers, an enforcement officer, a sheriff, a deputy United States Marshal, a Texas Ranger, a soldier and a man.

He doesn't even remember ever learning to ride a horse or even throw a lasso or handle a six-shooter. He just naturally did those things from the beginning, and horses in particular, he mastered in his early years.

Tom says that he did not have much education. Nevertheless, he has written splendid scenarios and lyrics, composed commendable music, and in addition to English, speaks Spanish and at least four distinct Indian dialects fluently. He received most of his early education from his brothers and sisters. Later they employed private tutors for him and finally shipped him off, at the age of fourteen, to the Virginia Military Academy, where he at once plunged into athletics and did horseback stunts that made his fellow students sit up and take notice.

The Spanish-American War in 1898 drove all thoughts of academic knowledge from Tom's mind and he enlisted in the Artillery. He was transported to Cuba and there received the baptism of fire at the Battle of Guaymas. Then he became a scout and was courier to General Chaffee, an old friend of his father. After the surrender in July of that year, Mix and other scouts were commissioned to round up Spanish Sharpshooters. In covering one of them who was hidden in a mango tree, Tom was shot in the mouth, the bullet coming out the back of his neck. This kept him a month in the hospital at Santiago, after which he was shipped home to the States, where he arrived about the middle of September. In a few short months he had graduated in first class warfare.

But Tom had gotten the taste of battle and soon he joined the provisional army for service in the Philippines. Then came the Boxer Uprising in China, where he was sent with the 9th Infantry in charge of a Gardiner Gun. He was with Colonel Listenn when the latter fell mortally wounded at the battle of Tien Tsing, and marched with the victorious allied army into Peking. During the fighting in China he was badly hurt and was sent home to the United States, being given an honorable disability discharge.

Later, he went to Denver to break horses for the British Government, and, finally, in search of further adventure, he sailed to South Africa with a load of horses during the Boer War. To be near war was to be in it, and presently Tom was in uniform again, taking part in the exciting doings around Ladysmith. He came back to the United States in 1903 and later assisted the famous Boer General Cronje in the reproduction of the Boer War spectacle at the St. Louis World's Fair.

Apart from the intervals in which he sought an education or pursued adventure in other lands, Tom Mix lived his life on the plains. He roamed the great western cattle belt, journeying from ranch to ranch, working here, there, and everywhere. He sojourned in Texas, Oklahoma, Colorado, Arizona, New Mexico, Wyoming and the two Dakotas.

It seems but natural to find such a man becoming a servant of the state—taking a hand in the preservation of law and order. He was known as a dangerous man with a six-shooter, although he seldom drew one in his own disputes unless forced to do so. He settled these with his fists, and he was generally victorious.

When he was elected sheriff of Montgomery County, Kansas, he made a complete success of the job and was later elected to the same position in Washington County, Oklahoma. Here, he and his deputies led the way in cleaning up that section of the country and driving out cattle thieves, outlaws and train robbers, and seldom came back from a man hunt empty handed. He was also a special enforcement officer of Eastern Oklahoma, which had been Indian Territory, and City Marshal of Dewey, Oklahoma. But these positions were too tame for Tom, who enlisted in the Texas Rangers.

At another time, in running down the leader of a gang of horse runners in New Mexico, he was badly wounded in the leg by a rifle bullet. Again, after a fight in which three men were killed, he himself was so badly wounded that doctors gave up all hope of saving him. But, he pulled through. Yet again, with Madero in Mexico, he was charged with a supposed violation of a military law, tried, condemned, and was actually facing a firing squad, when he was saved by the confession of a man who had testified against him.

It was in 1910 that the idea of going into motion pictures first occurred to him, partly as a result of seeing some imitation cowboys in a screen comedy, and partly through having been coaxed into performing some of his own stunts before a camera man.

Motion picture men had photographed him the year previous in Seattle, where he won the title of champion steer thrower of the world at the Alaska-Yukon-Pacific Exposition. He had reached the point in his career where sober judgement and cool calculation were

Mystery photo that probably inspired the legend that Tom was with Madero's forces in Mexico. (Courtesy Tom Mix Museum)

beginning to outweigh the sheer love of romance and adventure which had hitherto been the driving force that spurred him on. He figured that he had done his share of the rough work in the settlement of the great southwest and he calculated (with considerable business acumen) that the public would be interested in seeing a real cowboy doing real cowboy stunts on the screen.

So he went to Los Angeles and joined the movies. His first picture was *The Feud;* then came *Rough Riding Romance* and continuing in

Tom's boyhood interest in sports continued throughout his life. It was part of his physical fitness program. (Courtesy Tom Mix Museum)

this sort of photoplay, he soon became a popular hero of motion picture patrons the world over. During the filming of *Big Town Roundup,* he had several hair-breadth escapes from death, and in the *Speed Maniac,* he experienced more real speed than in any other race in his life. He seemed fond of real "hornet's nest" situations. In the picture of that name, the scenario of which he helped to prepare, he incorporated more of these situations than is usually included in the life of the average dare-devil.

In the multitude of successful motion picture productions for which he was afterwards responsible, Tom Mix not only became a star of stars, but also the best director in the business. It was he who directed the famous chariot race in *The Queen of Sheba,* which has never been surpassed.

Every patron of the motion picture theater knows Tom Mix and his wonder horse Tony, who for years have been almost inseparable. Millions have marveled at their daring feats and thrilled at the risks they ran.

Tom is the only master Tony ever had and the only person who has been on his back, which may partly account for their extreme love for each other. When Tom Mix went abroad in 1925, he naturally took Tony, the best known horse in the world, with him. The reception accorded them was by far the most extraordinary ever paid to American film celebrities in foreign lands. Record breaking crowds milled about them in the streets of European capitals, royalty greeted them with pleasure and Europe's newspapers treated them as official delegates at large from the United States. The old world recognized Tom Mix as a foremost exponent of clean, healthy entertainment and paid its homage accordingly. For Tom Mix pictures were always clean and he confined his productions to wholesome romance and adventure.

No finer example of clean living than Tom Mix walks the face of the earth. His life itself, as well as his pictures, has been a powerful influence for good in the lives of youth wherever the sun shines on civilization.

Almond-eyed children of Cherry Blossom Land, fur clad boys and girls of the steppes of Russia, swarthy sons and daughters of sunny Italy and Spain, sombrero decked youngsters of the Argentine, lads and lassies of bonny Scotland and millions of other children love Tom Mix. He is their champion and their love of him is just as intense as that of America's future citizens.

His fine health, the proper care he has taken of his splendid body— never giving it more fuel to take care of than it can—always keeping it tuned up to its finest pitch, has won the admiration of manhood everywhere. Danger and difficulty have never daunted him, nor broken bones deterred. He deems that part of the price to be paid for the honor and glory of his position, for the privilege of teaching youth to be honest and upright and strong and brave and clean, inside and out.

Race cars and motorcycles proved to be an interesting pastime for the nation's top star. (Courtesy Tom Mix Museum)

Boys realize that Tom Mix was once just an unknown American lad like themselves, and thousands upon thousands of them rely upon him as their model because they know he practices what he preaches. Who knows then but out of this great army of youth shall come not only one Tom Mix, but the Tom Mix of Maine, of Michigan, of Florida.

Fans and enthusiasts write to him from all corners of the globe. They name things after him, from babies to boots, and send presents for himself and Tony—and boys worship him.

Such in brief, is the man who asks your leave to be spokesman of the pioneers. He wishes to be quite sure that people will appreciate all that the cowboy and settler have done and what they have made possible. He is apprehensive that he may have not brought it all out in his pictures. Films may be forgotten, he thinks, when personal contacts are more enduring.

Tom kept his body in excellent physical condition and he frequently sparred with his trainer and boxing world notables. (Courtesy Tom Mix Museum)

Hence his desire to see and appear personally before this multitude of admirers, whose approbation made him the brightest star in moviedom's wild west firmament.

Tom's wish is now being fulfilled twice daily, when he and his famous wonder horse Tony appear in person before the audiences of the great Sells-Floto Circus.

After the end of the Tom Mix Circus venture and shortly before his death, Tom became more candid about his real life. In personal interviews, he talked about his Pennsylvania birth, denied his Indian blood, and even talked about settling down and "running for dog catcher." He also talked about serving with Batteries M and O of the 4th Regimental Artillery, saying that he had once been stationed near Portsmouth, New Hampshire. In a way, Tom seems to have been trying to put an end to the ten-headed dragon that had pursued him for over a quarter of a century. Unfortunately, Tom died before the dragon had been slain and a new series of legends popped up among the western novelists.

According to the new legend, Tom was really born Thomas Arthur Leventhau, the son of a Jewish, Italian, and French-Canadian miner. His birthplace was stated correctly, but his mother was now of gypsy, rather than Indian descent. From this point on, the story gets worse instead of better. Tom's mother, Elizabeth, particularly disliked the story about her being part Indian—undoubtedly, she would have been just as perturbed about the gypsy story!

If the legend of Tom Mix has been debunked, perhaps his spirit may now rest in peace. One sad aspect of the movie and circus legend is that its very existence casts doubt on those aspects of Tom's life which were in all probability quite true. There is little doubt that Tom favorably influenced the lives of thousands of young people and that he did his best to publicly represent those virtues which at one time were respected by most Americans.

12

A Summary of Thoughts

Tom's boyhood was typical of the times—he quit school at an early age as did many children for many years afterward. There was one important difference; Tom quit school not to go to work, but to dream and play. Tom was never really bad as a boy, but he just didn't like doing routine chores around the home. He was best described by his mother as, "just a big devil, too busy playing with guns to learn much." Tom was strong, alert, athletic-minded, spunky and persistent. He was determined to go West at a very early age. He lived to see the fulfillment of many of his childhood dreams. Without this great determination, he may have ended up as just another drifter or saddle bum. As a young man, Tom was tall (5'10"), broad-shouldered and dark complected. He made friends easily and he never outgrew the boyish Huckleberry Finn air that made him so popular. Tom's boyhood experiences may well have tended to make him overemphasize the importance of money in his later life. On the other hand, Tom never seemed to learn how to really manage the great sums of money he made.

While still in his teens, Tom was swept into a popular war by yet another dream—the dream of freeing an oppressed people from Spanish misrule. Once in service, he proved to be a natural leader. He was the one man who stood out among the crowd. In less than a year, he had been promoted to the rank of Sergeant; in less than two years, he was a First Sergeant. As a First Sergeant, Tom was the highest ranking noncommissioned officer in his battery. Tom

If this statue looks realistic to you, it's because Tom was clowning around again—this time on top of a war memorial. (Courtesy Tom Mix Museum)

enjoyed the privileges of rank and he enjoyed training new recruits. He was reputed to have been tough but fair in his dealings with the men under him.

Because of his position, Tom was able to keep his finger on the pulse of the Army. He knew and understood Army policy at a time when the country was engaged in the Spanish-American War, Philippine Insurrection, Boxer Uprising, and Boer War. What he lacked through personal experience, he picked up quickly from those veterans who were returning home. Soon Tom had heard so many tales that he could swap lies with the best of men. After all, it wasn't fashionable to be in the service and out of the action. Most of the little wars were short and there was a tremendous amount of turnovers and transfers. Soon, no one knew or cared if

Tom was a seasoned veteran or a lucky rookie. All that mattered was that he was a First Sergeant and the "big man in charge" of various operations. Tom was a success in his first big important role, that of a First Sergeant.

Tom finished his first three-year hitch with the Army and was honorably discharged at Fort Hancock, New Jersey. As a routine course of events, he immediately reenlisted and then took his furlough. Tom seems to have been intent on making a career of the Army at this stage of the game. At least, he didn't hesitate at all to sign up for a second three-year hitch.

One of the privileges of rank was the right of senior noncom officers to marry without obtaining the consent of the Commanding Officer, and that's exactly what Tom did. Grace was madly in love with her handsome, gallant First Sergeant and Tom had discovered that girls weren't so bad after all. Both of the young lovers soon learned that there was a big difference between courting and marrying. Once the honeymoon was over, there really wasn't much satisfaction in being married to a handsome, gallant soldier who was never home. Likewise, being a married man adds some new responsibilities to a well-regimented life.

Regardless of the circumstances, Tom's desertion is still a disappointment to any Tom Mix fan. After hearing tales of heroic deeds ever since 1910, it is extremely hard to believe that America's hero could have deserted his country for the whims of a mere female. The only consolation is that Tom had an honorable discharge which he justly earned and no man can take that away from him!

Tom's life seems to have been in a constant state of change for several years following "his failure to say good-bye to Uncle Sam." Apparently, he tried his hand at a number of jobs, becoming a physical fitness instructor, member of the Oklahoma Cavalry Band, and bartender. These jobs seemed to be just fill-ins until he got his big break, hiring on with the Miller Brothers' 101 Ranch. It seems natural that he would become interested in the Wild West Shows since Buffalo Bill was his first boyhood hero.

When Tom first hired on with the 101 Ranch, he wasn't heralded as being much of a cowboy. He had ridden horses as a boy and he had worked with them in the Army, but bronc busting, bulldogging, and steer riding were relatively new experiences for him. When Tom dressed up, he just naturally looked like a cowboy and he proved to be an excellent host for the eastern "dudes" who came to the ranch to vacation there. Everyone who met Tom liked him.

In a few short years, Tom improved his image as a cowboy, and soon he was able to hold his own with the best of them. It wasn't long before he teamed up with Bill Pickett and Stack Lee and was billed as one of the 101's champion cowboys. As his skills improved, his parts in the Wild West Shows grew. He began to enter the rodeo games for the sheer thrill and excitement of the sport. His athletic ability and agility, combined with his natural riding talents, enabled him to master cowboy sports in a minimum of time.

During his early motion picture career, Tom experienced a feeling of uncertainty. He enjoyed the Wild West Shows and the idea of performing for a live audience. The money from the movies seemed to come too easy and he wasn't sure that they were here to stay. The one thing that was certain was that the movies paid considerably more than the Wild West Shows. Perhaps Tom reasoned that he could always return to the Wild West Shows if things just didn't work out. But again, Tom was in the right place at the right time, and as the movies became popular so did he. By 1912, there was no question that the movies were here to stay!

To say that Tom was a total abstainer would be foolish in the light of the material previously presented. Shooting lemons out of shot glasses on Saturday night and honky-tonkin' around the mining towns doesn't conform very well to the theory that Tom never drank or smoked. In real life, Tom did both, but not to excess. Tom enjoyed an occasional drink with Buster Keaton and other Hollywood notables. He hit the bottle a little hard during the later years, when his circus got into financial troubles and his old friends started dragging him through the courts. Even then, Tom seemed to have a remarkable ability to pull himself up by his own bootstraps. In interviews, Tom was careful to state that he never drank or smoked while on the screen. He really believed in setting a good example for youngsters watching his movies.

Tom's personal life had its ups and downs. His first two marriages didn't last long. Tom was probably as much to blame for this as anyone else, as he was known to have an eye for the pretty girls. His marriage to Olive Stokes appeared to have many of the lasting qualities not found in his first two marriages. Olive was attractive and she could take her "little boy" in tow when the situation called for it. A daughter, Ruth, was born and for a time it appeared that the couple might settle down in a little dream ranch in Arizona. But Tom's rapid rise to fame kept pushing back his

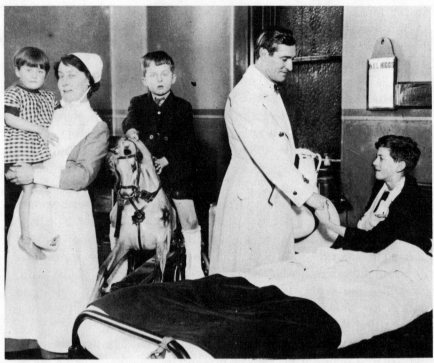

Tom visiting a crippled children's hospital. (Courtesy Tom Mix Museum)

dreams of settling down. Olive had plenty of competition among Tom's ever-present leading ladies. Tom settled for a career rather than a permanent family. In later life, he seemed bitter about his inability to make a success out of marriage. Once he casually remarked, "When a man's been married half a dozen times, any sentiment about anniversaries is as cold as the ashes of last year's campfire. Payin' all them alimonies sorta drowns out the romance."

In the twenties, Tom Mix and Victoria Forde enjoyed unprecedented worldwide fame. They shared the same glass bubble that was destined to break during the stock market crash. During his years of fame, Tom spent his money almost as fast as he made it. He lived in true Hollywood style. Everything he had was the best that money could buy. He dressed lavishly, sporting a diamond-studded belt buckle and diamond-studded spurs. He had a fine collection of horses, guns, and saddles. Tom continued to live in a dream world and he threw away great sums of money.

Tom always enjoyed personal contacts with people. The doors of his mansion home were always open to friends. Tom once said

Tom Mix was the first big star to work on fund-raising drives for the needy. (Courtesy Tom Mix Museum)

that he personally "knew more theater owners, politicians, school teachers, and Boy Scouts, than any man alive." An outright boast perhaps, but not too hard to believe.

There are numerous stories about Tom taking the time to visit with friends in need. Such was the case with master Georgie Wood, age 12, who received a serious back injury, was hospitalized, and then confined to bed. Tom learned about the boy through his friends. On one Friday morning in September 1928, Tom called on the boy at his home in Peru, Indiana.[1] After Tom was greeted at the door by the boy's parents, he strolled into the boy's bedroom and said, "Howdy, lad." The man and the boy talked and joked, as if they had been pals all of their lives. Tom talked of returning with Tony in the fall, and later, the boy's father remarked, "I wouldn't care if Tom brought Tony right into the house and put him in the other bed next to Georgie's; that's what I think of that big-hearted cowboy. He and Tony can come any time, day or night—they'll always be welcomed as long as I've got a home."

Tom also had a soft spot in his heart for animals. He had always loved horses; dogs and bears didn't seem to be exceptions either. On several occasions, the Humane Society presented Tom with awards. Tony was his horse and Tag was his dog. Other animals were also frequently used in Tom Mix movies. In each movie where an animal was used, a strong friendship was allowed to mature between the man and animal. This theme, of course, was very popular with youngsters.

A good many Tom Mix movies were directed toward the younger generation. Youngsters themselves were often featured in Tom's movies and many of yesterday's youngsters, who are today's elderly men, remember working with Tom and Tony. These men admired Tom and his horse as boys and will fondly remember them until their dying days. In one of Tom's last pictures for Universal, entitled *My Pal, The King*, Mickey Rooney played the part of a boy king, who had never seen a real Wild West Show. The movie is complete with cowboys and Indians, and in the plot Mickey is rescued from an evil Count by Tom.

A good many other Hollywood stars gained a small amount of acclaim after they appeared in a Tom Mix movie. Barbara LaMarr, Colleen Moore, Billy Dove, Clara Bow, Laura LaPlante and Ann Pennington were among the heroines whose careers were boosted by appearing with Tom. George O'Brien, a former cameraman with Tom's production crew, later became a western star as did John Wayne, who was once a "prop boy" on the Mix set. George and John saw Tom in action and evidently they "learned a few tricks of the trade."

The depression years of the early thirties marked the turning point of Tom's career. Although he was far from finished, and still

1. Based on a story from *The Peru Republican*.

Mix's movies appealed to a youthful audience. The following scenes are from My Pal, the King. *(Author's collection)*

Tom's wild west show comes to a foreign land.

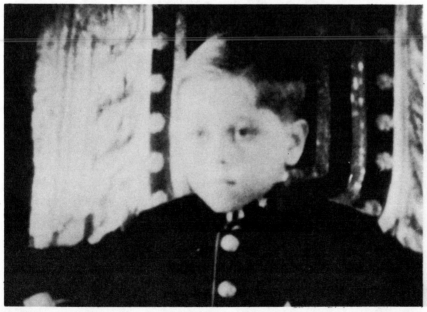

Boy King, Mickey Rooney, about to sneak off to see the big parade.

Mix rushing to boy's rescue after he is abducted by the crooked count.

Mix drops in on the crooked count . . .

. . . takes him in tow . . .

. . . and rescues the boy king.

amassed considerable wealth after that time, things were never quite the same for the former Fox superstar. Tom lost about a million dollars in the stock market crash; he was plagued by illness, injury and numerous law suits. In spite of all this, Tom made a couple of moderately successful movie comebacks and was featured with the Sells-Floto Circus for three years.

The beginning of the end came when Tom invested about $400,000 of his savings in the Sam B. Dill Circus which he took out on the road as the Tom Mix Circus. The venture was marked by disaster after disaster, and in three short years it had to close because operations were no longer profitable. Tom's daughter, Ruth, was a comfort in these trying days and she co-starred with her father in what was to become his last great venture.

Professional people in the entertainment business remember Tom Mix as one of the greatest showmen of all times. Tom played his part well. The white Stetson hat, fancy-buttoned shirts, custom-fitted trousers, and hand-carved boots may not have been typical cowboy garb, but they set the standards for the industry for years to come. Ken Maynard, Gene Autry, and Roy Rogers were just three successors who followed in Mix's footsteps as far as dress is concerned. The second thing which comes to mind is Tom's riding ability. Many people agree that the combination of man and horse has never been equalled. Tom and Tony performed their stunts in a dramatic and believable fashion.

If there was one thing for which Tom deserved more credit than he received, it would be for promoting cowboy sports. Tom participated in Wild West Shows, frontier day celebrations, and later organized rodeos. Unfortunately, there are few written records existing prior to 1912 to document Tom's activities in this field. But Tom's sphere of influence seems to have brought him in touch with all of the cowboy sports champions who were active in this field in the early 1900s.

Tom Mix has always been considered more or less as a man of mystery. Perhaps this is because he was discreet about his personal life. On the other hand, part of the mystery was probably caused by the contradictory legend of Tom Mix. At this late date, it is extremely difficult to distinguish between Tom's legendary acts of heroism and true life adventures. The legend of Tom Mix will probably never die; it has survived for too many years!

In summary, it must be said that Tom Mix was an outstanding screen personality and a very great man. His image inspired loyalty

Tom Mix and Tony set the standards for future generations of western stars.

to the point of blind devotion. No one ever seriously questioned the legend of Tom Mix until long after his death. Tom's lectures on law and order, motherhood, and the American flag were sincere on his part and believed by those who heard him. He sincerely believed that youngsters should be Straight Shooters in life and strive to do their best in all of their undertakings.

Many people, even those who cooperated in furnishing material for this story, may be somewhat disillusioned by this new picture of Tom. Nevertheless, the information presented has been carefully researched and in most cases, verified by one or more highly reliable sources. It would have been Tom's wish for some of the future Tom Mix's of the world to pursue their dreams to a highly successful conclusion, while striving to avoid many of the pitfalls of a legendary hero who has gone before them.

Appendix

BIBLIOGRAPHY OF CREDITS

The author wishes to thank and acknowledge the persons and organizations listed in this bibliography. It would have been impossible to write this book and its story without the help of many personal friends and living friends of Tom Mix. The author wishes to extend a special thanks to Mrs. Frankie Barr Caldwell for the family history of the "Mix Clan," to Mr. Francis P. Clark of the University of Notre Dame for researching most of the motion picture and circus work material, and to the Tom Mix Museum of Dewey, Oklahoma for the excellent collection of rare and interesting photographs which appear in this book.

Arizona
Florence Chamber of Commerce
Mr. Bob Hanesworth
Pinal County Historical Society
Mr. Don Stillman

California
The California State Library
Mr. Robert Hazelleaf

Colorado
Mr. Raymond M. Beckner
Colorado Springs Chamber of
   Commerce
Mr. David Hardy
Mr. Lonnie Higgins

Pikes Peak Regional Library

Delaware
Fort Delaware Society
The Hagley Museum
Mr. Douglas C. West

Indiana
Mr. Francis P. Clark
Miami County Historical
   Museum

Iowa
Blackhawk Films
Mrs. Mildred Mix Marek

Kentucky
The Louisville Times

Missouri
The Ralston Purina Company

Oklahoma
Mr. Jack C. Baskin
Blackwell Chamber of
  Commerce
Col. Bailey C. Hanes
Mr. Gareth Muchmore
The Oklahoma Historical
  Society
Ponca City Chamber of
  Commerce
Tom Mix Museum, Inc.
Will Rogers Memorial
  Commission
National Cowboy Hall of Fame

Pennsylvania
Cameron County Historical
  Society
Mrs. Frankie Barr Caldwell
Mr. John E. DuBois Jr.
Mr. W. T. Evans
Mr. Chester B. Hall
Pa. Historical and Museum
  Commission

Mr. John J. Pentz
The John B. Stetson Co.
Mrs. Mae Mix Thomas

South Carolina
Mr. & Mrs. Paul D. Mix
Mrs. Leona Frontroth
The Honorable J. Strom
  Thurmond

Virginia
Fort Monroe Casemate Museum

Washington, D.C.
National Archives and Records
  Service
United Spanish War Veterans
The Library of Congress

Wisconsin
Circus World Museum

Canada
Glenbow-Alberta Institute
The Medicine Hat Historical
  and Museum Foundation

England
Mr. John M. Hall

*Tom Mix Films of The Selig Polyscope Company (all silent)**

1. The Wilderness Mail   (1914—2 reels)
2. Moving Picture Cowboy   (1914—2 reels)
3. Shooting up the Movies   (2 reels)
4. Tom's Strategy
5. Making an Impression
6. Along the Border   (1916)

* Release dates and number of reels shown in parentheses when known.

  7. Making Good
  8. On the Eagle's Trail
  9. A Mix-up in the Movies
 10. A Corner in Water
 11. A Bear of a Story
 12. The Pony Express   (2 reels)
 13. A Western Masquerade
 14. The Passing of Pete
 15. Cactus Jim's Shop Girl
 16. The Sheriff's Duty
 17. Going West to Make Good
 18. Taking A Chance
 19. A $5000 Elopement
 20. The Range Rider   (1910)
 21. Back to the Primitive   (1911)
 22. Escape of Jim Dolan   (1913)
 23. Local Color   (1916)
 24. An Arizona Wooing   (1915)
 25. Cactus Jim   (1915)
 26. Taming of Grouchy Bill   (1916)
 27. Ranch Life in the Great Southwest   (1910)
 28. Crooked Trails   (1916)
 29. In the Days of the Thundering Herd   (1914)
 30. Mrs. Murphy's Cook
 31. Chip of the Flying U   (1914)
 32. Sagebrush Tom
 33. In Defiance of the Law   (3 reels)
 34. The Raiders
 35. The Heart of Texas Ryan   (1916)
 36. Twisted Trails   (1916—2 reels)
 37. The Wagon Trail
 38. Pals in Blue
 39. The Stage Coach Driver
 40. The Man from Texas
 41. Single Shoot Parker
 42. Foreman of the Bar Z
 43. Days of Daring
 44. Legal Advice
 45. Up San Juan Hill   (1910)
 46. Briton and Boer   (1910)
 47. Millionaire Cowboy   (1910)

48. An Indian Wife's Devotion   (1910)
49. Tom's Sacrifice
50. The Sheriff's Girl
51. Why the Sheriff Is a Bachelor
52. Mr. Haygood Producer
53. Pony Express Rider
54. Weary Goes Wooing
55. Roping a Sweetheart
56. The Outlaw's Bride
57. The Heart of a Sheriff
58. The Parson Who Fled West
59. Saved by Her Horse
60. A Militant Schoolman
61. Getting a Start in Life
62. The Scapegoat
63. Saved by a Watch
64. The Rival Stage Lines

Tom's Selig Films were classified as western drama, comedies, and
features.

Leading Ladies	Popular Male Players
Kathlyn Williams	Charles Clary
Myrtle Steadman	Pat Chrisman
Victoria Forde	Bill Duncan
Bessie Eyton	Sid Jordan
	Joe Ryan

Tom Mix Films for William Fox Productions (all silent)

1918
  1. Cupid's Roundup
  2. Six Shooter Andy
  3. Western Blood
  4. Ace High

1919
  5. Fame and Fortune
  6. The Wilderness Trail
  7. Hell Roarin' Reform
  8. Fighting for Gold
  9. Coming of the Law

1920
10. Desert Love
11. The Daredevil
12. The Cyclone
13. The Speed Maniac
14. The Terror
15. The Feud
16. Three Gold Coins
17. The Untamed
18. Mr. Logan, U.S.A.
19. Treat 'Em Rough
20. Rough Riding Romance

1921
21. Hands Off
22. Prairie Trails
23. A Riding Romeo
24. The Road Demon
25. The Texan
26. Big Town Roundup
27. The Night Horseman
28. After Your Own Heart
29. The Rough Diamond
30. Trailin'

1922
31. Sky High
32. Chasing the Moon
33. Up and Going
34. The Fighting Streak
35. Four Big Streaks
36. Just Tony
37. Do and Dare
38. Tom Mix in Arabia
39. Catch My Smoke

1923
40. Romance Land
41. Three Jumps Ahead
42. Stepping Fast
43. The Lone Star Ranger
44. Soft Boiled
45. Mile a Minute Romeo
46. North of Hudson Bay
47. Eyes of the Forest

1924
48. Ladies to Board
49. The Troubleshooter
50. The Heartbuster
51. The Last of the Duanes
52. Oh You Tony
53. Teeth

1925
54. The Deadwood Coach

55. Riders of the Purple Sage
56. The Rainbow Trail
57. The Lucky Horseshoe
58. The Best Bad Man
59. The Everlasting Whisper
60. Dick Turpin

1926
61. The Yankee Sen'or
62. My Own Pal
63. No Man's Gold
64. Hardboiled
65. The Great K and A Robbery
66. The Canyon of Light
67. Tony Runs Wild

1927
68. The Circus Ace
69. Outlaws of Red River
70. Silver Valley
71. Tumbling River
72. The Arizona Wildcat
73. The Bronco Twister
74. The Last Trail

1928
75. Horseman of the Plains
76. Hello Cheyenne
77. Daredevil's Reward
78. Painted Post

Leading Ladies

Marlow Nixon
Essie Ralson
Alma Bennett
Betty Jewel
Claire Adams
Colleen Moore
Sylvia Joceln
Alice Spencer
Claire Anderson
Billy Dove

Tom Mix Films of the Film Booking Office (all silent)
Year released—1929

Titles	Leading Ladies
The Drifter	Sally Blaine
The Dude Ranch	Dorothy Dwan
The Big Diamond Robbery	
King Cowboy	
Outlawed	
Son of the Golden West	

Tom Mix Sound Films for Universal Pictures

Titles	Release Date
Destry Rides Again	April 17, 1932
Rider of Death Valley	May 26, 1932
Texas Bad Man	June 30, 1932
My Pal, the King	August 4, 1932
The Fourth Horseman	September 29, 1932
Hidden Gold	November 3, 1932
Flaming Guns	December 22, 1932
The Terror Trail	February 2, 1933
Rustler's Roundup	March 3, 1933

Tony Jr. was introduced in the Universal films.

The Tom Mix Mascot Serial—The Miracle Rider (1935), sound,
featuring Tony Jr.

Episode Titles
1. The Vanishing Indian
2. The Firebrand Strikes
3. Flying Knives
4. A Race With Death
5. Dougle-Barreled Doom
6. Thundering Hooves
7. The Dragnet
8. Guerilla Warfare
9. The Silver Band
10. Signal Fires
11. A Traitor Dies
12. Danger Rides With Death
13. The Secret of X-94
14. Between Two Fires
15. Justice Rides The Plains

Episode 1., 5-reels; other episodes, 2-reels each.

Cast

Tom Mix: Tom Moran
Joan Gale: Ruth

Charles Middleton: Zaroff
Jason Robards: Carlton
Bob Kortman: Longboat
Edward Earle: Adams
Edward Hearn: James
Tom London: Sewell
Niles Welsh: Metzger
Edmund Cobb: Vining
Ernie S. Adams: Stelter
Max Wagner: Morley
Charles King: Hutton
George Chesebro: Crossman
Jack Rockwell: Rogers
Stanley Price: Chapman
George Burton: Mort
Tony Jr.: Tony Jr.

TOM MIX RADIO SHOW (1933–1950)

The role of Tom Mix was played by various actors during this period: Artells Dickson, Russell Thorson, Jack Holden, and Curley Bradley.

Producer: Al Chance

Director: Charles Claggett

Writers: George Lowther
Roland Martini
Charles Tazewell

Theme: "When It's Roundup Time in Texas and the Bloom is on the sage."

Radio Time: Monday through Friday: 15-minute serial. Monday, Wednesday, and Friday: 30-minute complete story.

Premiums: In 1935, a book similar in format to the old Big Little Book series was offered. It was entitled, *The Trail of Terrible 6* and was free for one box top. Written on the first page was, "To my loyal and faithful Straight

Shooter Pals, who are now over a million strong, I dedicate this book, [signed] *Tom Mix.*"

In 1936, a Tom Mix six shooter, which was a replica of Tom's gun, was offered for one boxtop and ten cents. The gun was wooden, painted black with ivory-white handles.

In the forties, a series of comics were issued. The first nine issues were published under the title of *Tom Mix Comics.* With the tenth issue, the title was changed to *Tom Mix Commando Comics,* with Tom and his gang fighting everything from outlaws to an army of invisible invaders and a squadron of real flying dragons from Japan.

Ralston Jingle #1*

When its Ralston time at breakfast
Then it surely is a treat
To have some rich, full-flavored Ralston
Made of golden western wheat.

Wrangler says it is DEEEE-LICIOUS
And you'll find before you're through
With lots of cream—Boy it sure tastes keen
It's the tops for breakfast too.

Ask your mother in the morning
To serve you up a steaming plate
It's a grand, hot, whole wheat cereal
And the cowboys think its great.

Once you try it, you'll stay by it
Tom Mix says it's swell to eat.
Jane and Jimmy too, say it's best for you
Ralston cereal can't be beat!

* Ralston Jingles and Straight Shooter's Pledge reprinted by courtesy of The Ralston Purina Company of Checkerboard Square.

Ralston Jingle #2

Shredded Ralston for your breakfast
Starts the day off shining bright;
Gives you lots of cowboy energy
And a flavor that's just right.

It's delicious and nutritious,
Bite-sized and ready-to-eat,
Take a tip from Tom,
Go and tell your mom
Shredded Ralston can't be beat!

Ralston Straight Shooter Pledge

I promise to shoot straight with my parents by obeying my father and mother.

I promise to shoot straight with my friends by telling the truth always, by being fair and square at work and play, by trying always to win, but being a good loser if I lose.

I promise to shoot straight with myself by striving always to be at my best, by keeping my mind alert and my body strong and healthy.

I promise to shoot straight with Tom Mix by regularly eating good old Hot Ralston, the official Straight Shooter's cereal, because I know Hot Ralston is just the kind of cereal that will help build a stronger America.

TOM'S PERSONAL APPEARANCE TOUR (ENGLAND,
1938–39 SEASON)

September 5th—London Palladium
          12th—London Palladium
          19th—Birmingham Hippodrome
          26th—Liverpool Empire

October   3rd—Nottingham Empire

10th—Sheffield Empire
17th—Leeds Empire
24th—Glasgow Empire
31st—Edinburgh Empire

November 7th—Sunderland Empire
14th—Newcastle Empire
21st—Hull Palace
28th—Ilford Hippodrome

December 5th—Brighton Hippodrome
12th—Finsburgh Park Empire

January   23rd—Wolverhampton Hippodrome

February 6th—Holloway Gaumont
13th—Portsmouth Hippodrome
20th—Holborn Empire
27th—Chiswick Empire

April   10th—Mandreder Hippodrome

MICROFILM RECORDS

Reel #1—161 Double Frames on 35mm film.

Frame #   *Description*

1. Tom Mix in *Cactus Jim's Shop Girl.*
2. General movie ad
3. Tom Mix in *Twisted Trails.*
4. Tom Mix in *Tom's Strategy.*
5. Tom Mix in *Shooting up the Movies.*
6. Tom Mix in *A Corner in Water.*
7. Tom Mix in *On the Eagles Trail.*
8. Tom Mix in *Making Good.*
9. Tom Mix in *Making Good.*
10. Tom Mix in *The Raiders.*
11. Tom Mix in *Going West to Make Good.*
12. Tom Mix in *The Sheriff's Duty.*

13. Tom Mix in *Taking a Chance, A $5000 Elopement.*
14. Tom Mix in *The Passing of Pete.*
15. Tom Mix in *A Western Masquerade, A Bear of a Story.*
16. Tom Mix in *The Pony Express.*
    (All of the above items filmed from 1916 newspapers.)
17. List of Tom Mix Fox Films.
18. List of Tom Mix Selig Films.
19. Selig Reviews
20. Selig Reviews
21. Universal, Mascot, & F.B.O. Films.
22. Article on Sid Jordan
23. Rev. of F.B.O. Film, *Son of the Golden West.*
24. Rev. of F.B.O. Film, *Outlawed.*
25. Rev. of F.B.O. Film, *King Cowboy.*
26. Rev. of F.B.O. Film, *The Drifter.*
27. Rev. of Fox Film, *Fame and Fortune.*
28. News item on powder burn to the eye.
29. News item on shoulder injury.
30.–32. News items on injuries and lawsuits.
33. News items on Vicky Forde Mix divorce.
34. News item on escape with death.
35. News item on custody of daughter, Thomasina Mix.
36. News item on injuries.
37. Tom's statement on "saving the nation."
38. Article on Tom's death.
39, 40. New York Times Obituary.
41. Los Angeles Times Obituary.
42. Associated Press Release about Tom's death.
43. Universal Film movie ads.
44. Ad of Tom's first Selig picture, *Ranch Life in the Great South-West* (1910).
45. Tom Mix in *Days of Daring.*
46. Tom Mix in *Twisted Trails, Wagon Trail, Pals in Blue, The Stage Coach Driver, The Man from Texas, Single Shot Parker* and *Foreman Bar Z.*
47. Reviews of *The Foreman of the Bar Z, The Wagon Trail, Twisted Trails* and *Pals in Blue.*
48. Tom Mix in *The Feud.*
49. Tom Mix in *The Untamed.*
50. Tom Mix in *3 Gold Coins.*

51. Tom Mix in *The Daredevil.*
52. Tom Mix in *Desert Love.*
53. Tom Mix in *The Speed Maniac.*
54. Tom Mix in *The Cyclone.*
55. Tom Mix in *Prairie Trails.*
56. Tom Mix in *The Texan.*
57. Tom Mix in *The Road Demon.*
58. Tom Mix in *Stepping Fast.*
59. Tom Mix in *Do and Dare.*
60. Tom Mix in *Arabia.*
61. Tom Mix in *Sky High.*
62. Tom Mix in *Catch My Smoke.*
63. Tom Mix in *Soft Boiled.*
64. Tom Mix in *North of Hudson Bay.*
65. Tom Mix in *Romance Land* with Billie Dove.
66. Tom Mix in *Lone Star Ranger* with Billie Dove.
67. Tom Mix in *Soft Boiled.*
68. Tom Mix in *The Mile-A-Minute Romeo.*
69. Tom Mix in *3 Jumps Ahead.*
70, 71. Tom Mix in *Eyes of the Forest.*
72. Tom Mix in *Heart Buster.*
73. Tom Mix in *The Last of the Duanes.*
74. Tom Mix in *The Trouble Shooter.*
75, 76. Tom Mix in *Ladies to Board.*
77. Tom Mix in *Teeth.*
78. Tom Mix in *Pals in Blue.*
79. Tom Mix in *Riders of the Purple Sage.*
80. Tom Mix in *The Everlasting Whisper.*
81. Tom Mix in *Dick Turpin.*
82. Tom Mix in *The Best Bad Man.*
83. Tom Mix in *The Rainbow Trail.*
84. Tom Mix in *The Deadwood Coach.*
85. Tom Mix in *The Lucky Horseshoe.*
86. Tom Mix in *The Canyon of Light.*
87. Tom Mix in *My Own Pal.*
88. Tom Mix in *No Man's Gold.*
89. Tom Mix in *Tony Runs Wild.*
90. Tom Mix in *The Great K & A Train Robbery.*
91. Tom Mix in *The Yankee Senor.*
92. Tom Mix in *Hard Boiled.*

93. Tom Mix in *The Bronco Twister*.

94. Tom Mix in *Outlaws of Red River*.

95. Tom Mix in *The Circus Ace*.

96, 97. Tom Mix in *The Last Trail*.

98. Tom Mix in *Silver Valley*.

99. Tom Mix in *King Cowboy* by F.B.O.

100. Tom Mix in *The Drifter* by F.B.O.

101, 102. Tom Mix in *The Big Diamond Robbery* by F.B.O.

103. Sells Floto Circus—1929.

104. Tom Mix in *Texas Bad Man* by Universal.

105. Tom Mix in *Rider of Death Valley* by Universal

106. Tom Mix in *The Miracle Rider*—1935 serial by Mascot.

107. 1930 Sells Floto Circus Ad and article by Tom entitled "Mix Urges Sunday School."

108, 109. Sells Floto Circus.

110, 111. 1934 Sam B. Dill Circus

112. 1935 Tom Mix Circus.

113. 1936 Tom Mix Circus and article, "Tom Mix Deplores Softness in Modern Generation."

114, 115. Tom Mix Circus

116. News item on shoulder being rewired.

117, 118. News item on lawsuits.

119. Injuries and court cases.

120. 1935 article, "How I Broke into the Movies" by Tom Mix.

121. 1934 lawsuit with the Miller Brothers.

122. 1935 announcement about returning to the screen.

123. 1937 Ruth Mix in the movies.

124, 125. Peru, Indiana Obituary.

126. Article, "There Was a Cowboy" by John Hall.

127, 128. Tom Mix in *Screen Oddities*.

129. Ruth Mix films, *The Little Boss, The Girl from Oklahoma*.

130. Ruth Mix and Rex Bell in *The Tonto Kid*.

131. Article, "Gene Autry."

132–134. Article, "Tom Mix" by Johnny Mack Brown.

135, 136. *Movie Thrills* Magazine. (1950)

137. Article on Buck Jones.

138. Article on Tom Mix.

139. Article on Harry Carey.

140. Shazam Magazine article.

141–144. Article, "Tom Mix the Miracle Rider" by Jim Harmon.

145–150. Article, "Tom Mix" by George Mitchell & Wm. Everson.

151, 152. *Los Angeles Times* obituary.

153–156. Article, "Tom Mix the Celluloid Cowboy" by Norman Katkov.

157. *Man* Magazine Cover.

158–161. Article, "Tom Mix, The Greatest Cowboy of Them All" by William C. Thompson.

Microfilms Reels 2 & 3; Regimental returns of the 4th U. S. Artillery and 48th Company, Coast Artillery Corps.

*Partial Genealogy of the "Mix Clan."**

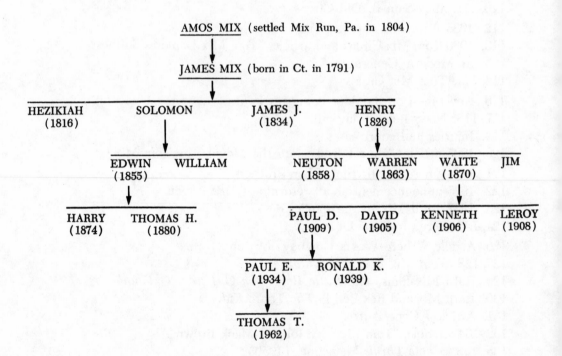

* Most members of the Mix family should be able to trace their family history from the information presented above.

The family of Amos Mix and the Overturf family came up the Susquehanna River by Rafts from Lockhaven to settle Mix Run in 1804. James married one of the Overturf girls.

The sons and daughters of James Mix were Hezikiah, Solomon, James J., Henry, Annaliza, and Nancy.

The daughters of Hezikiah Mix were Anna and Clara.

The sons and daughters of Solomon Mix were Emma, Jean, William and Edwin (Tom's father).

The sons and daughters of James J. Mix were Catherine (called Kate), George A., John, and Laura.

The sons of Henry and Lydia Mix were Newton, Warren, Waite, Jim and Leonard Dill (a stepson).

The sons and daughter of Annaliza Mix and Benjamin Smith were Julia, Ella, Issac, and James.

The sons and daughters of Nancy Mix and Allen Barr were James, Marshall, Flora, and Merritt.

Index